Apress Pocket Guides

Apress Pocket Guides present concise summaries of cutting-edge developments and working practices throughout the tech industry. Shorter in length, books in this series aims to deliver quick-to-read guides that are easy to absorb, perfect for the time-poor professional.

This series covers the full spectrum of topics relevant to the modern industry, from security, AI, machine learning, cloud computing, web development, product design, to programming techniques and business topics too.

Typical topics might include:

- A concise guide to a particular topic, method, function or framework

- Professional best practices and industry trends

- A snapshot of a hot or emerging topic

- Industry case studies

- Concise presentations of core concepts suited for students and those interested in entering the tech industry

- Short reference guides outlining 'need-to-know' concepts and practices.

More information about this series at https://link.springer.com/bookseries/17385.

Engage, Excel, and Elevate with Microsoft Viva Engage

Transform Your Organization Through Communities and Conversations

Charles Waghmare

Apress®

Engage, Excel, and Elevate with Microsoft Viva Engage: Transform Your Organization Through Communities and Conversations

Charles Waghmare
Matunga, Mumbai
Maharashtra, India

ISBN-13 (pbk): 979-8-8688-0765-7   ISBN-13 (electronic): 979-8-8688-0766-4
https://doi.org/10.1007/979-8-8688-0766-4

Managing Director, Apress Media LLC: Welmoed Spahr
Acquisitions Editor: Malini Rajendran
Development Editor: Laura Berendson
Coordinating Editor: Smriti Srivastava

Cover designed by eStudioCalamar

Distributed to the book trade worldwide by Apress Media, LLC, 1 New York Plaza, New York, NY 10004, U.S.A. Phone 1-800-SPRINGER, fax (201) 348-4505, e-mail orders-ny@springer-sbm.com, or visit www.springeronline.com. Apress Media, LLC is a California LLC and the sole member (owner) is Springer Science + Business Media Finance Inc (SSBM Finance Inc). SSBM Finance Inc is a Delaware corporation.

For information on translations, please e-mail booktranslations@springernature.com; for reprint, paperback, or audio rights, please e-mail bookpermissions@springernature.com.

Apress titles may be purchased in bulk for academic, corporate, or promotional use. eBook versions and licenses are also available for most titles. For more information, reference our Print and eBook Bulk Sales web page at http://www.apress.com/bulk-sales.

Any source code or other supplementary material referenced by the author in this book is available to readers on GitHub (https://github.com/Apress). For more detailed information, please visit https://www.apress.com/gp/services/source-code.

If disposing of this product, please recycle the paper

"The fear of the LORD is the beginning of knowledge"
– Proverbs 1:7

I would like to express my heartfelt gratitude to the Almighty Lord Jesus Christ for giving me yet another opportunity to author this book. I owe everything to Him and I am so grateful for all the good things that He has done in my life. God Bless.

My Dedication

Over a year following the demise of my dearest mother, late Mrs. Kamala David Waghmare, I have penned this book. I dedicate this book to my dearest mother and to my father, Mr. David Genu Waghmare, who both laid the foundation of my life and career. Without them, I am nothing. I thank God for the best mom and dad.

Also, I dedicate this book to my adorable wife, Mrs. Priya Waghmare, for her support, love, encouragement, and care.

Table of Contents

About the Author

 **Charles David Waghmare**, presently a DBA (Doctor of Business Administration) scholar from the prestigious SP Jain School of Global Management, as well as an MBA from the same prestigious B-School, has over 17 years of industry experience in IT, engineering, and energy sector.

Charles is presently working with a global energy leader since 2019 as an Information and Records Management Consultant in the Microsoft 365 space. Before that, he worked for Capgemini for eight years in various roles, including Viva Engage Community Manager and Manager of the Drupal-based Enterprise Knowledge Management system. He also developed a knowledge management platform for Capgemini's Digital Customer Experience (DCX) organization using SharePoint Online to manage client references and knowledge assets related to artificial intelligence and customer experience (CX). Further, he adopted Microsoft Azure Chatbots to automate communication channels with customers.

Charles also worked for SIEMENS Information Systems Limited for five years. During his tenure there, he was a Community Manager of SAP-based communities, where he utilized TechnoWeb 2.0 – a Viva Engage–like platform – and on-premises SharePoint to manage SAP user–based communities. Also, Charles was the global rollout manager for a structured document management system built in on-premises SharePoint.

Charles has penned several books on Microsoft 365 technologies such as Viva Engage, SharePoint Online, Azure Chatbots, and also on ChatGPT. Further, he loves reading motivational books in his spare time, his favorite being *The Monk Who Sold His Ferrari and The 5 AM Club*.

About the Technical Reviewer

 **Kapil Bansal** is a PhD Scholar and Lead DevOps Engineer at S&P Global Market Intelligence, India. He has more than 15 years of experience in the IT industry, having worked on Azure cloud computing (PaaS, IaaS, and SaaS), Azure Stack, DevSecOps, Kubernetes, Terraform, Office 365, SharePoint, release management, application lifecycle management (ALM), Information Technology Infrastructure Library (ITIL), and Six Sigma. He completed certification programs in Advanced Program in Strategy for Leaders from IIM Lucknow and Cyber Security and Cyber Defense from IIT Kanpur. He has worked with companies such as IBM India Pvt Ltd, HCL Technologies, NIIT Technologies, Encore Capital Group, and Xavient Software Solutions, Noida, and has served multiple clients based in the United States, the UK, and Africa, such as T-Mobile, World Bank Group, H&M, WBMI, Encore Capital, and Bharti Airtel (India and Africa). Kapil also reviewed *Hands-On Kubernetes on Azure: Run your applications securely and at scale on the most widely adopted orchestration platform* and *Azure Networking Cookbook: Practical recipes to manage network traffic in Azure, optimize performance, and secure Azure resources* published by Packt and many more as well as *Practical Microsoft Azure IaaS: Migrating and Building Scalable and Secure Cloud Solutions* and *Beginning SharePoint Communication Sites* published by Apress and many more.

Acknowledgments

I would like to remember the following people who are close to my heart:

Late Mr. Anil Malvankar, ex-DGM at SIEMENS, who offered me my first job at SIEMENS. I thank him for his mentoring until his last day on this earth, April 2024.

Late Mr. Alwin Fernandis, my beloved friend. He is not present with me today, but his memories exist in my heart forever.

Mr. Sridhar "Sri" Maheswar, supply chain consultant, NNIT. I am always grateful for your support, my beloved friend.

Mr. Pravin V. Thorat, Head of India Operations at ATOS. I thank you for your prayers and good wishes.

CHAPTER 1

Introduction to Viva Engage: Understanding the Platform

The Viva Engage platform brings people together to connect with one another and with their communities. It allows individuals to share their experiences and ideas and find belonging at work. Viva Engage is part of Microsoft's employee experience platform. It enables organizations to connect and discover their purpose and insight. In this introductory chapter on Viva Engage, we will introduce Viva Engage to understand the platform, the potential rebranding from Yammer, a description of Viva Engage features, a few use cases, and how Viva Engage fits into the broader Microsoft 365 ecosystem.

Introduction

Due to the increasing number of hybrid and remote work environments, employees have less time to connect with one another and their organizations. To improve the quality of their work experience, leaders need to create a new environment that is designed to meet the expectations of their employees. Building strong relationships is the most challenging aspect of remote and hybrid work. Social capital is also important for organizations to succeed.

With the launch of Microsoft Viva Engage, employees can now feel included in the company's culture and be their best. Through Microsoft Viva Engage, leaders can now shape the culture of their organizations by connecting with their employees and making them feel valued and included. It's built on the foundation of the company's social networking platform, Yammer. It allows people to connect with their colleagues and find answers to their questions.

Viva Engage is a collaboration social platform that enables people to connect with each other and express themselves through conversations and digital communities. It builds on the capabilities of Microsoft 365 and Teams. Leaders can easily share ideas, discuss strategy, and interact with their employees using Viva Engage. It offers various features such as virtual events and pinned conversations, notifications across multiple platforms, and more.

With Viva Engage, employees can build professional networks and communities, share their perspectives, and get answers to their questions. Its features, such as storylines, help encourage participation and develop relationships with colleagues.

Through the storyline feature, Viva Engage allows you to share your perspective with your organization. Using storyline, you can create rich posts that include photos, videos, and links. These can be used to reach and engage your followers and colleagues in various platforms, such as Microsoft Teams.

The Storylines tab also features a feed of content from people you follow. You can also create short videos or photos to share with your colleagues and friends. Viva Engage is a part of Microsoft's Viva suite, which is designed to provide an enjoyable work experience. Existing Microsoft 365 customers can download the app for free, and users who have Yammer license can access Viva Engage (Figure 1-1).

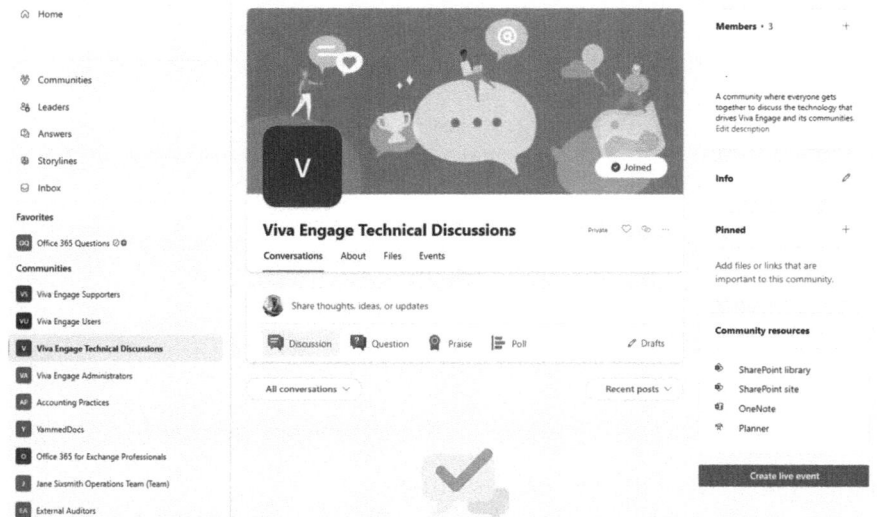

Figure 1-1. *Home page of Viva Engage*

Top Features of Viva Engage

The Viva Engage platform delivers a variety of high-quality experiences for employees, such as community building, self-expression, and knowledge sharing. It is available on all of Microsoft's platforms, including Office 365 and Windows 10. The Viva Engage platform has some awesome features that connect employees, managers, and leaders to create, share with, and engage communities. The following are some of the awesome features of Viva Engage which makes social collaboration simple and easy.

Communities: The goal of a community as shown in Figure 1-2 is to provide a central place for employees to share their thoughts and experiences, as well as for company-wide communications. It can be private or public in nature.

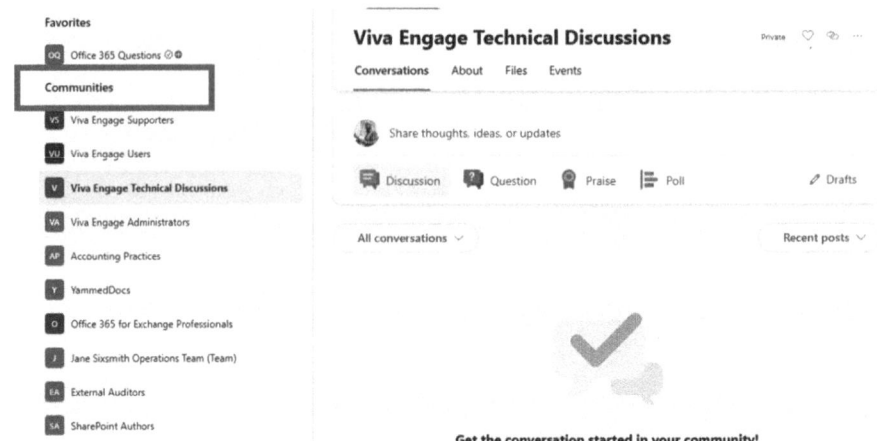

Figure 1-2. *Viva Engage communities*

Announcements: Community administrators can make announcements so that the entire community can know about important information. When this happens, members will be notified via email in Viva Engage. They can also change their preferences for notification.

To make sure that users understand the importance of announcements, use it sparingly. The announcement feature is shown in Figure 1-3. Also, keep in mind that the delivery time increases as the audience gets bigger. For instance, if you want to notify a group of 50 users, it might take around a few minutes, but it can take several hours to send to 100,000.

Figure 1-3. *Announcement in Viva Engage*

Keep in mind that announcements are not designed to be used for emergencies. Instead, they should be short and contain a clear call to action. Also, plan to link to other important topics so that the community can get the most out of them. Finally, allow users to ignore announcements that are less urgent or when there are multiple high-impact ones being made simultaneously.

Conversations: Post questions, comments, polls, and discussions in your community or on your personal story as shown in Figure 1-4. You can also add photos, videos, and other media files through a media editor. To type a message, select the publisher window located anywhere. Tag people (using @mention) who will find the post interesting or helpful. You can also use a hashtag to promote the message, so others can discover it. Share photos, videos, and documents to make your post more collaborative and contextual. Alternatively, add a GIF to emphasize your message. You can also attach a file, tap to like and share comment on a published conversation.

Figure 1-4. *Conversation in Viva Engage*

Home Feed: One of the most important factors that employees can consider when it comes to keeping up with the news in their company is keeping up with what's happening in their team. The goal of the Viva Engage home feed is to drive engagement and discovery across storylines and communities. It uses algorithms to identify the most relevant posts to you based on your interests. Each person's home feed is different, and it personalizes the experience by analyzing all of the messages that you see in it.

The home feed of Viva Engage is designed to provide you with the latest news and updates about your organization. It's also useful for keeping track of what your team and other individuals are talking about.

The home feed as shown in Figure 1-5 displays the most recent conversations that you're likely to encounter on topics that are relevant to you and your network. The communities that you're connected to include those that you're a part of, those that you've seen messages from, and those that you've shared content with.

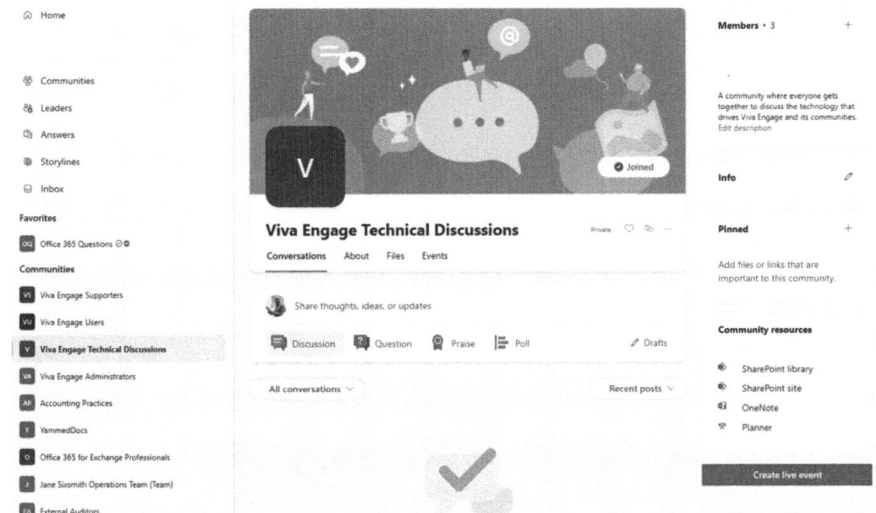

Figure 1-5. *Home feed in Viva Engage*

The people that you're close to use data from Viva Engage and Microsoft 365. They include individuals who have posted messages you've liked or responded to, people you've chatted with through private messages, and individuals you've invited to groups. Recently posted messages that have garnered a lot of likes or replies are known as "trending messages" and are also viewed in the home feed.

Virtual Events: You can also host a live video event that features interactive Q&A sessions and Viva Engage conversations. As shown in Figure 1-6a, live events can be created and produced for people using Viva Engage, which feature built-in discussions that can be used before, during, or after the event. You can allow up to 10,000 people to attend at the same time, and you can make a video available afterward so that those who can't make it to the event can still participate.

7

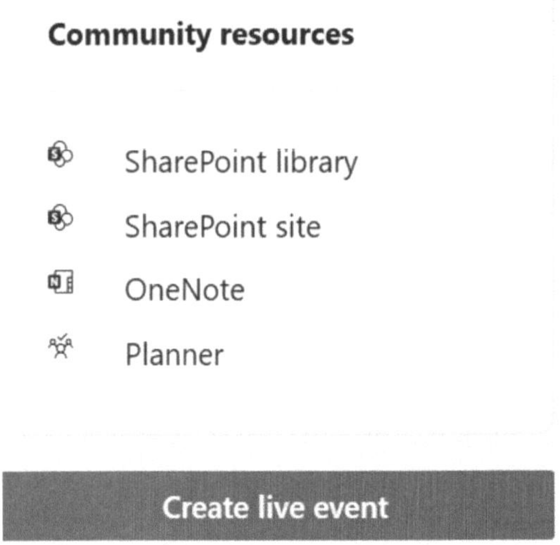

Community resources
SharePoint library
SharePoint site
OneNote
Planner
Create live event

Figure 1-6a. *Live Event creation button in Viva Engage*

Virtual events are created with the help of seamless integration between Viva Engage and Microsoft Teams as shown in Figure 1-6b. When you select the Create live event option in Viva Engage, you actually get redirected to MS Teams for event creation.

Collaboration best practices
Queue
Live event
Live event will resume in a moment

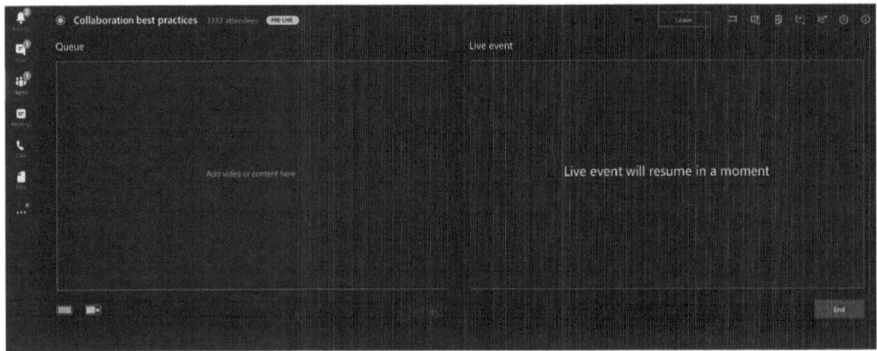

Figure 1-6b. *Live Event creation in MS Teams*

Q&A and Best Answers: In Viva Engage communities, users can ask and answer questions to help others improve their knowledge as shown in Figure 1-7. Post your own answer and earn points for it. The community admin or the member who posted it can also mark it as the best answer, which appears at the top.

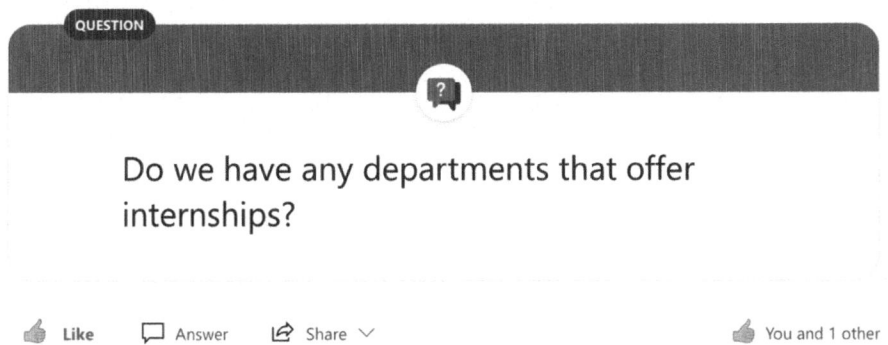

Figure 1-7. Live Event Q&A in Viva Engage Communities

Storyline: Share your thoughts and ideas to help others improve their skills and experience. As shown in Figure 1-8, you can also post and share content to your network of followers and other individuals from within your company. People who want to know what you've shared can visit your profile page to see what's happening in Viva Engage, Teams, and Outlook.

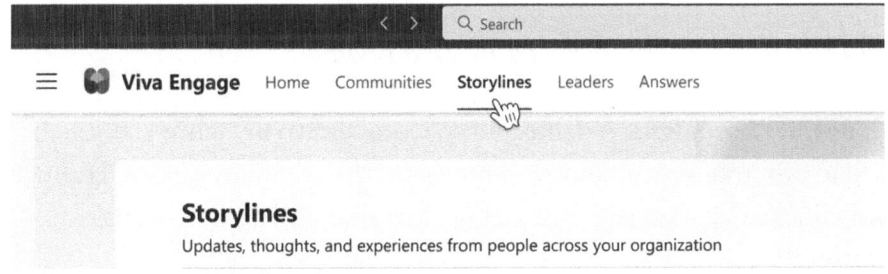

Figure 1-8. Storylines in Viva Engage

In Viva Engage, you can start the conversation with the people around you. Your storyline will allow you to share your experiences, discuss your interests outside of the office, and celebrate milestones. The Storylines tab will let you know what people are talking about in your company.

Leadership Corner: Leaders can encourage open communication within their teams and communities through AMA (Ask Me Anything) events, surveys, and news as shown in Figure 1-9. In Viva Engage, the leadership corner is where you can stay up to date with the latest content posted by your leaders. It also lets you discover communities they've joined and ask them questions directly through their AMAs. This feature gives you the necessary tools to build strong connections with your leaders.

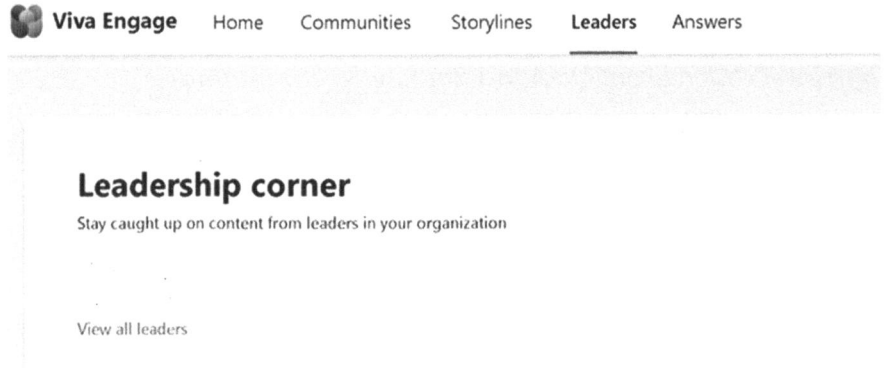

Figure 1-9. *Leadership corner in Viva Engage*

Social Campaigns: A dedicated space as shown in Figure 1-10 can be used to promote key initiatives that support the company's goals. Through campaigns in Viva Engage, you can get involved and build a stronger community.

Figure 1-10. *Social campaign corner in Viva Engage*

There are two types of campaigns available through Viva Engage. One of these is an official campaign, which is created by your organization's Microsoft 365 global admin. The other is a community campaign, which is created by the community admins. To post to community campaigns, members can use the campaign hashtag on the publisher window of either the campaign page or the community page. For the official campaign, you can directly post from the home feed.

Answers in Viva: The new conversational platform known as Answers in Viva enables large organizations to interact with each other and learn from one another. It uses natural language processing to match questions to existing and crowdsourced answers, and it rewards individuals who contribute to the platform.

Employees can improve their knowledge and connect with other experts by asking questions through Answers as shown in Figure 1-11.

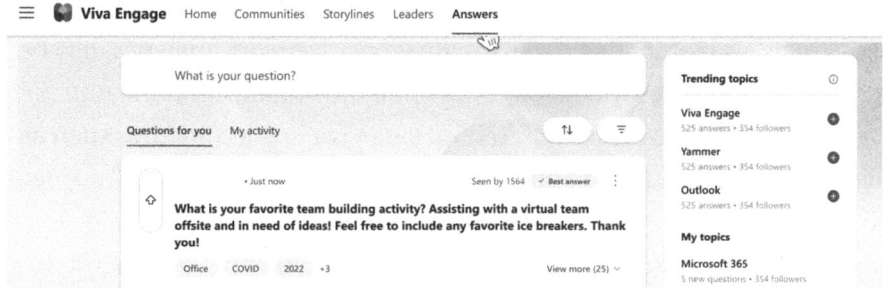

Figure 1-11. *Answers in Viva in Viva Engage*

Advanced Analytics: With the ability to view different metrics such as My Analytics and Org Analytics, you can get a deeper understanding of the trends and engagement within Viva Engage as shown in Figure 1-12. With Viva Engage, you can easily monitor the impact of your posts. Its robust analytics platform will let you know how your content is perceived.

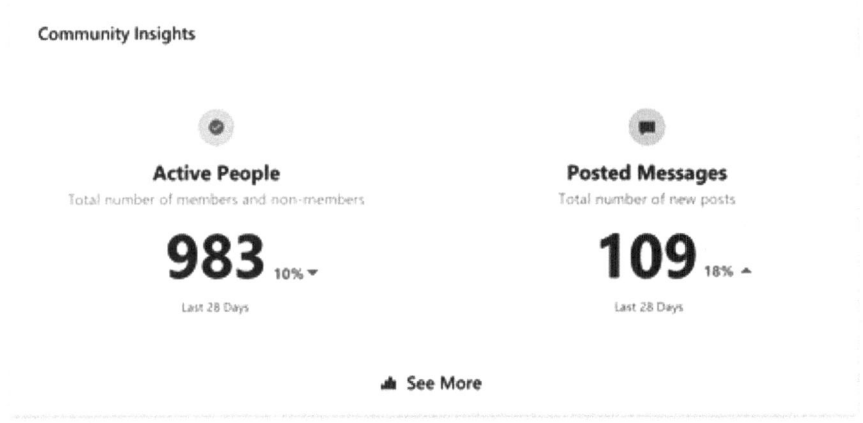

Figure 1-12. *Community analytics in Viva Engage*

Through your conversations, answers, and personal data, you can monitor and improve your engagement. Community analytics is a tool that lets you monitor and improve your engagement in various communities. With the help of Viva Engage, you can analyze and measure the reach and engagement of your community. You can also learn more about the individuals and topics that make up the group. Network analytics may be activated for your network depending upon the organizational setup.

In this section, we have covered various Viva Engage features such as communities, announcements, conversations, home feed, virtual events, Q&A and best answers, storyline, leadership corner, social campaigns, Answers in Viva, and advanced analytics. Each feature creates a modern digital experience to build a collaborative and connected organization, thereby increasing organizational productivity.

Rebranding from Yammer to Viva Engage: Farewell Yammer, Welcome Viva Engage

Microsoft has been a long-time supporter of the development of Yammer, which was first introduced in 2008. It is publicly known that Yammer was acquired by Microsoft more than a decade ago in 2012 for $1.2 billion. Although some companies have had a hard time adopting it, others have been able to use it to drive engagement and knowledge sharing.

One of the main strengths of Yammer is its ability to be easily integrated into a SharePoint intranet. It's a great choice for organizations that want to manage their communities. In addition, it's more effective than Microsoft Teams when it comes to project and team collaboration. As per a general announcement by Microsoft, the rebranding of its social networking platform from Yammer to Viva Engage is not a complete goodbye for Yammer, but it will remain the same as before, and Microsoft will continue to provide the same features and investments for its customers. In addition, the company is planning on releasing new features in the platform in the future with a brand-new name, Viva Engage.

Meaning of Rebranding

The rebranding of Microsoft's enterprise social network, known as Yammer, is a significant step in the company's evolution. It also represents a change in the company's approach to addressing the digital workplace.

Reduced Confusion

The rebranding of Yammer Communities to Viva Engage had many people scratching their heads. It involved the dual branding of the product, which confused end users and digital workplace teams. With the whole thing, the company was able to reduce the confusion and provide a more straightforward message. In response to the confusion, Microsoft through its public announcements acknowledged that the dual brand had caused some issues. They said that it had been challenging to create a clear and consistent message for end users.

Lift Viva Brand

Two years ago, Microsoft launched the Viva brand. Although end users are aware of its name due to the email summaries that they receive, it is still not widely used in the digital workplace. Most of the adoption of Viva has been around its Connections app, which is paid for.

The company's decision to change the name of its social networking platform, from Yammer to Viva Engage, is intended to make the brand more visible to both end users and its stakeholders. It also allows people to experience the company's offerings outside of Microsoft Teams.

New Features Launched

When a company rebrands, it usually involves communicating with its users and stakeholders, but it also focuses on the new features that are designed to make the platform more social. For instance, with the new features that were introduced recently, Viva Engage became much more like Meta's Workplace.

In late 2022, the company introduced storylines and stories, which are features that allow people to post as individuals and have people follow them. This move away from being primarily focused on communities and groups shows that Viva Engage is more about people. Meanwhile, stories are short videos and photos that are similar to TikTok and Instagram. The new features will be highlighted in the company's rebranding.

Viva Engage Notifications Through Teams

It is inevitable that there will be some effort to explain the new look and feel of Viva Engage to end users. This is an additional task that most digital workplace teams will probably find very challenging. However, it is also an opportunity to reinforce the value of the features of the platform. Microsoft has provided a schedule that shows when the main changes will happen and how they will affect the various applications. In addition, they are also providing in-app messages to inform users about the rebrand.

Development of Premium Features

Prior to being bundled with Microsoft 365, Yammer was also included with Viva Engage. The rebranding of Yammer to Viva Engage allowed the company to introduce a variety of new features in 2023, such as enhanced leadership communications. These paid-for features can be easily positioned under the Viva brand, as they are already different from what's included in a standard Microsoft 365 license.

Only subscription-based users will be able to enjoy the following new features within Viva Engage:

- The leadership corner is a place where leaders can connect with their employees. It features discussions and content.

- AMA events is a template that enables senior managers and leaders to conduct interactive events using Viva Engage.

- Internal communicators can now create and manage social media campaigns that work seamlessly with the leadership corner using Viva Engage.

- The new features of Viva Engage include a series of advanced dashboards that allow users to analyze their campaigns and audience engagement.

- A feature known as the Answers in Viva, which is integrated with the Viva Topics, allows users to ask questions.

There has always been a question about Microsoft's investment in Yammer, but the company has started to actively invest in the platform in the past couple of years. The new features that have been added to Viva Engage show that the company is committed to making it a part of its long-term plans.

Microsoft's decision to change the name of its platform from Yammer to Viva Engage is an opportunity to educate users about the various features it has to offer. We believe that it will continue to add value to the digital workplace.

Viva Engage Use Cases

The following describes the various use cases for Microsoft's Viva Engage, which aims to help organizations improve their collaboration and communication.

Employee Recognition

One of the most effective ways to improve employee productivity and morale is by recognizing them for their achievements. With Viva Engage, managers can easily post achievements and milestones on social media. They can also acknowledge contributions by awarding digital badges. For instance, if an employee completes a major project, their achievements can be publicized by their peers and team. This type of recognition can boost a person's morale and encourage a culture of appreciation.

In addition, Viva Engage can be utilized to carry out regular pulse surveys, wherein the goal is to gather feedback on certain issues. This allows organizations to gain a deeper understanding of their staff members' sentiments. For example, a company may use Viva Engage to gather insights about its employees' experiences after it introduced a work-from-home policy.

Internal Communication

Viva Engage is a tool that allows organizations to share important announcements and updates. These can include product or service changes, financial results, holiday schedules, and changes in policies. For instance, if a company decides to launch a new software, it can create a series of posts on the platform explaining how it will benefit its employees.

Through Viva Engage, employees can easily connect with one another and work on cross-functional projects. For instance, a marketing team might use the platform to connect with an individual in the product development department to learn about how to improve the effectiveness of marketing campaigns.

Knowledge Sharing and Collaboration

Through Viva Engage, communities can be created that are focused on specific areas or topics. These allow members to share knowledge and collaborate on best practices. For instance, a project management community can discuss issues and share templates. This type of interaction can help build a repository of knowledge for anyone in the organization.

Groups in Viva Engage can be created for teams that are working on projects. These can be used to keep track of progress, share documents, and talk about project-related issues. Groups can also be used by product launch teams to organize tasks and keep track of updates.

Training and Onboarding

New employees can take advantage of Viva Engage's onboarding tools to ask questions, access resources, and connect with mentors. It helps them feel supported and welcomed. For instance, finance department employees can join a community to learn more about the company's processes and find answers to their inquiries.

Employees can easily share training materials and other resources through Viva Engage. They can also ask questions and get help from trainers or peers. For instance, following a cybersecurity training, participants can converse in Viva Engage to talk about their experiences and share tips on how to improve their daily functions.

Events and Campaigns

Internal campaigns, such as charity drives or wellness initiatives, are commonly conducted by organizations. With Viva Engage, they can easily communicate details about these efforts, as well as engage participants. For instance, staff members can share photos of their activities and post their achievements during a wellness challenge.

Through Viva Engage, event organizers can promote and organize internal workshops, webinars, and other internal events. They can also create groups and events to keep their employees engaged. For instance, a department may hold a quarterly town hall using the platform to share the agenda and collect questions from their employees before the event.

Crisis Communication

One of the most critical factors that businesses consider when it comes to implementing a communication strategy is ensuring that their employees are aware of the latest updates. With the help of Viva Engage, leaders can easily disseminate important information to their employees in real time. For instance, during a natural disaster, they can use the platform to provide updates on the status of the company's safety measures and other support services.

Employees can establish support communities in Viva Engage to connect with one another and share resources during times of crisis. For instance, during an outbreak, a community can help workers discuss health guidelines and other wellness topics.

Executive Engagement

Through Viva Engage, leaders can reach out to their employees and share their vision for the company. It also allows them to interact with two-way dialogues. For instance, a CEO can post regularly updates about the company's performance and strategic initiatives, and employees can ask questions.

Through Ask Me Anything (AMA) sessions, leaders can provide employees with answers to their questions directly in Viva Engage. These sessions can also help them address their concerns and provide insight into certain issues. For example, they can hold a discussion about an organization's recent changes after announcing them.

Cultural and Social Initiatives

One of the most important factors that employers can consider when it comes to creating an inclusive work environment is supporting initiatives that promote diversity and inclusion. Through groups in Viva Engage, employees can discuss their experiences with these topics and share resources. For instance, a women's network group can use this platform to talk about the challenges that women face in the workplace and create events to celebrate their achievements.

Through Viva Engage, workers can create interest groups and social clubs that help them connect with others who share similar interests. For example, a book club may use the platform to promote its offerings and share reviews. This type of social interaction can help develop a sense of belonging and community.

Detailed Example: Implementing Viva Engage in a Mid-Sized Tech Company

Scenario: A tech company with about 2000 employees uses Viva Engage to improve its internal communication and employee engagement. The firm's workforce is spread across different locations globally.

This use case focuses on enhancing the **recognition of employees**. With Viva Engage, the HR department can create a Star Performer program that allows employees and managers to nominate their colleagues who have gone beyond their duties. The program then allows the entire company to celebrate and recognize the achievements of the nominated individuals. It also helps boost the employee's morale and encourages them to excel at their work.

In the second use case, Viva Engage is used to facilitate **internal communication** within the organization. The company's management team uses Viva Engage to regularly post updates about the company's performance and upcoming projects. This method allows employees to ask questions and comment on the posts, which keeps them engaged and informed.

This use case aims to create **knowledge sharing communities**. The various divisions of Viva Engage create communities to share knowledge and collaborate on various tasks. For instance, the software development group's community is dedicated to sharing ideas about new technologies and coding techniques. Likewise, the marketing division's forum is used to discuss market trends and brainstorm creative strategies. These communities can serve as valuable learning tools.

This use case is to help organizations seamlessly **onboarding and training** their employees. The HR division of Viva Engage has a community that's designed for new hires. This area allows them to connect with their peers and access onboarding materials. In addition, it hosts live Q&As with the company's representatives. This also lets new hires ask questions and get help from the HR department.

The next use case is in the coordinating of **internal campaigns**. Every year, the company holds an innovation challenge, where staff members are encouraged to submit their ideas for process improvements and new products. The campaign is managed through Viva Engage, which allows employees to discuss their suggestions with their coworkers and vote on the ones that they like the most. The judges then choose the winning proposals. This campaign promotes a sense of involvement and creativity among the staff.

The next use case covers the management of **crisis communication**. The IT department utilizes Viva Engage to keep its employees informed about the status and expected response time of a network outage. Regular updates are provided on a regular basis, and workers can ask questions or report issues. This type of communication lets employees manage their expectations and lessen the frustration they feel during a crisis.

Another use case is about fostering **leadership communication**. The company's CEO holds regular live Ask Me Anything (AMA) sessions in Viva Engage, where employees can ask questions and receive direct answers from the organization's leader. These sessions promote a culture of trust and openness, making workers feel valued and heard.

This use case is about supporting **diversity and inclusion initiatives**. The firm launches a dedicated group in Viva Engage that aims to promote inclusion and diversity. This section allows members to share their personal experiences and learn more about diverse practices. Moreover, the group organizes events like cultural celebrations and workshops, which can help improve the working environment.

The final use case is to **facilitate social connections**. Through social clubs in Viva Engage, employees can connect with others based on their shared interests. These groups can also plan activities and share tips. These tools help employees develop connections outside of their workplace.

Viva Engage and Microsoft 365 Ecosystem

As part of its Viva suite, Microsoft's Viva Engage is designed to help organizations improve their collaboration, communication, and engagement. Its integration with the company's other offerings can help them create a more seamless and personalized digital workplace. This exploration looks into how Viva Engage can be used to enhance the overall Microsoft 365 ecosystem.

Integration with Microsoft Teams

The main hub for collaborating within Microsoft 365 is Microsoft Teams. With Viva Engage, users can easily access various social features and engagement capabilities from within the team environment.

The integration of Viva Engage into Teams makes it easier for users to access its features without having to change applications. This feature will allow employees to stay informed about the latest developments in the company, as well as participate in social communities.

Users can now easily share announcements, posts, and updates within Teams. This feature will help promote a more collaborative and cohesive environment within the company. For instance, a project team using Viva Engage can talk about achievements and milestones within their channel.

Integration with SharePoint

One of the most powerful tools for collaboration and content management is Microsoft SharePoint. With Viva Engage, you can add social features and community elements to enhance the experience of using this platform.

With the addition of a social layer, such as through comments and likes, to a SharePoint site, users can interact with the content more easily. This allows them to gain deeper insight into the organization's resources and improve their productivity. For instance, a department might have a site that is dedicated to project management and document sharing. With Viva Engage, they can easily add social features to this site.

The social features of Viva Engage enhance the capabilities of SharePoint, allowing users to easily share their documents and pages within the platform's communities. This integration enables organizations to break down silos and ensure that their valuable content is easily accessible.

Integration with OneDrive

Cloud storage company OneDrive provides a variety of file sharing and storage capabilities. Its integration with Viva Engage enables users to collaborate and share documents across the company's social media platform.

Through the integration of OneDrive with Viva Engage, users can easily share files stored in the cloud with their colleagues. This feature makes it easier to share presentations, documents, and other files among people. For instance, an employee can easily share a report about a project within the company's community, which is dedicated to best practices in project management.

With the integration of Viva Engage and OneDrive, users can now work on documents in real time while also participating in the discussions within the platform. This makes it easier for them to carry out their tasks and improve their efficiency.

Integration with Outlook

Microsoft Outlook is the primary application used by users of Microsoft 365. With Viva Engage, users can stay connected to their email while keeping their engagement levels high.

Notifications are sent by Viva Engage to notify users about important updates and community posts. They are also sent directly to their Outlook inboxes so that they can keep up with all the activities happening within the app.

Users can sync their events and activities with Outlook, so they can keep track of all the activities happening in the app. This feature also helps in managing their schedules and prevents them from missing important training sessions, webinars, or community events. For instance, a town hall event that's scheduled in Viva Engage can automatically appear in the users' calendars.

Integration with Power Apps

The Power Platform of Microsoft includes various tools such as Power BI, Power Automate, and Power Virtual Agents, which can help organizations make informed decisions and improve the efficiency of their operations.

With the Power BI platform, organizations can visualize and analyze their data. Through the integration of Viva Engage and Power BI, they can create and share interactive dashboards and reports within their communities. For instance, a sales team can discuss their monthly sales performance through an embedded Power BI dashboard.

Through the Power Apps platform, companies can create custom applications that can be integrated with Viva Engage. For instance, a company can create a recognition app that will help track employee points and improve the effectiveness of its recognition programs.

Workflow automation can be enabled with the Power Automate feature, which allows companies to create processes that work seamlessly with Microsoft 365 tools, such as Viva Engage. For instance, an organization can automate the sending of congratulatory messages to employees after they complete Viva Learning courses.

Virtual agents can be created through the Power Virtual Agents feature, and they can be integrated with the Viva Engage platform to provide employees with automated support. For example, a chatbot in Viva Engage can help individuals navigate through various tasks and obtain information.

This covers the description of Microsoft 365 services with Viva Engage which aims to achieve powerful social collaboration and knowledge sharing within communities with the help of Do-It-Yourself technologies as described in this section.

With this, we have come to the end of the introductory chapter on Viva Engage. In this chapter, we have covered an introduction to Viva Engage to gain understanding of the platform, its potential rebranding from Yammer, a description of Viva Engage features, a few Viva Engage use cases, and how Viva Engage fits into the broader Microsoft 365 ecosystem. The next chapter will focus on driving user adoption and engagement with Viva Engage among employees at all levels of the organization, including communication plans, training programs, and incentivization approaches and creating and nurturing communities within Viva Engage. So, stay tuned!

CHAPTER 2

Strategies for Driving User Adoption of Viva Engage

After taking a deep dive into the Viva Engage platform, its features, a few Viva Engage use cases, and the Viva Engage and Microsoft 365 ecosystem in the previous chapter, we will take a deep look at and learn practical steps and best practices for implementing Viva Engage within your organization. In this chapter, we will primarily cover some basic understanding of user adoption such as why it is need, its benefits and how it can be implemented. Further we will also cover how to drive user adoption and engagement with Viva Engage across all employee levels in the organization. Building Viva Engage communication plans and training programs, with incentivization approaches will also be covered. Finally, we will provide guidance for communities creation and its nurturing.

Introduction

What Is User Adoption?

The process of user adoption refers to the learning curve that enables people to use a new technology or system in an organization. It is very important that a new initiative is successful because the effectiveness of a tool is directly linked to how well its users use it. The initial step in the process of user adoption is to provide a comprehensive overview of the new system, which will help them understand its benefits. This step is followed by a variety of educational opportunities that will help them improve their skills. Some of these include workshops, webinars, and tutorials.

Consistent and clear communication is also important, as it lets users know about any changes or updates while also highlighting the advantages of the tool. Change management techniques can help alleviate resistance by explaining how their implementation will improve workflows. A variety of support structures, such as dedicated support teams and help desks, are available to help users navigate through the system and resolve their issues. Self-help guides and documentation also provide helpful details. Feedback mechanisms can help an organization understand how the tool functions and make improvements.

Developing communities of like-minded individuals fosters collaboration and the exchange of best practices, making the user experience more enjoyable. Metrics and analytics-based monitoring can help determine if additional support is required and assess how the tool affects productivity. Adopting new technology and systems should be carried out in a way that makes them an integral part of the organization's daily workflows. Doing so can help boost the company's efficiency and success.

Why Do We Need User Adoption?

The adoption of new technology and systems is very important for organizations as it directly affects their return on investment (ROI) and effectiveness. Even the most advanced technology can fail to deliver its intended value if it is not adopted properly. There are many factors that can be considered when it comes to adopting new technology, such as improving productivity and maintaining a competitive advantage. The cost of implementing new technology is significant. Organizations spend a lot of time and resources trying to acquire, deploy, and maintain new systems. Without the proper adoption of such technology, they are not able to achieve their goals. Having the highest level of user adoption is very important to ensure that the organization can maximize its ROI.

User adoption can increase efficiency and productivity. New technologies and tools are often introduced to help organizations improve their processes and make better decisions. For example, a CRM system helps sales teams track and manage their customers. If the sales team doesn't adopt a CRM system, they might continue using inefficient techniques, which can lead to data inconsistencies and decreased opportunities. Having the proper user adoption process can help boost the efficiency of the organization. One of the most important factors that organizations consider when it comes to adopting new technology is ensuring that their users are comfortable with the new system. This can be done using effective adoption strategies that address the various concerns of their users. This can help minimize the disruption to their daily operations. Having the proper training and support can help them adapt to the new system quickly.

The culture of innovation can also be fostered by the availability of new technology. When workers are receptive to new innovations, they are more inclined to embrace other improvements and enhancements. This mindset serves as an encouraging trait for companies in today's competitive environment. A company can find that its workers are more inclined to try new digital tools after successfully implementing a new collaboration platform. By being more willing to try new innovations, an organization can take advantage of market changes and grow its competitive advantage. High levels of user adoption are also important in maintaining a competitive advantage. Today's fast-paced environment requires companies to continuously improve their capabilities and processes. Organizations that can successfully implement new technology can differentiate themselves by delivering better customer experiences and by introducing innovative services and products.

The adoption of new technology can also help organizations improve the accuracy of their data. Modern systems often have extensive capabilities when it comes to analyzing and collecting data. For instance, an ERP system can help organizations manage their various business processes. The value and accuracy of data collected depend on the consistent usage by each user. Without the full adoption of an ERP system, errors and inaccuracies can lead to poor decision-making and analysis. This is why it is important that employees adopt the system right away. Having the proper adoption can help organizations achieve their goals and improve their efficiency.

The morale and satisfaction of workers can also be improved by having the proper training. This can help them feel more positive about the changes and see the benefits of the new system. Unfortunately, if the adoption rate is poor, employees might feel frustrated, have difficulty accepting the changes, and might even start to resist the new technology. In the case of a time-tracking system that lacks proper support and training, employees might find it hard to use, leading to a decrease in their morale. Adoptive strategies aim to make workers feel more competent and confident when using new technology, thereby improving their job satisfaction.

The adoption of new technology also plays an important role in ensuring that the company's operations are secure. Modern systems often have features designed to help prevent unauthorized access and use of their data. If users fail to adopt the system, an organization may end up exposing itself to compliance violations or security breaches. By making sure that everyone correctly uses the system, an organization can ensure that it is following relevant regulations.

Adoptive strategies must involve several elements. One must ensure that all users are trained on the new system, with ongoing refresher courses available as needed. Clear communication must also be maintained, as it will help them understand how the change will benefit them and the company. Having the proper support structures also helps organizations improve the efficiency of their operations. These include support networks, help desks, and user guides. These provide the necessary resources to help users fully utilize the system.

One of the most important factors that organizations must consider when it comes to adopting new technology is the availability of feedback mechanisms. Through active engagement, they can identify issues early, as well as make necessary changes to address them later. This process can help the system remain relevant and functional. Creating communities of users allows them to share their ideas and provide each other with valuable feedback. Measuring and monitoring the adoption of a new technology through performance metrics and usage analytics can provide organizations with valuable insight into how the system is being used. These reports can help them identify areas where they might need to provide additional support.

User adoption is an essential part of any organization's strategy when it comes to implementing and using new technologies. It can help boost the company's productivity, improve its competitive advantage, and ensure seamless transitions. Organizations can achieve high levels of adoption by focusing on the following aspects: training, support, and communication.

What Are the Benefits of User Adoption?

The adoption of new technology is a critical part of any organization's success. It involves the acceptance of a new process or technology by end users, who will be using it daily. There are a variety of unique benefits associated with end-user adoption:

- One of the most important advantages of adopting new technology is its ability to improve the efficiency and productivity of end users. They will be able to perform tasks more accurately and efficiently, which can reduce their time and resources.

31

- The ROI of an organization increases as more end users adopt and utilize a new technology. This is because the company benefits from the increased efficiency and productivity that the system provides.

- The reduction of resistance to change can be achieved by end-user adoption. This can be achieved by training the end users on how to use the new technology.

- The adoption of new technology can also lead to an increase in end-user satisfaction. This can be achieved by the end users' positive experiences with the new system.

- Besides, the adoption of new technology can also lead to better decision-making. This can be achieved by having more data collected and used in the decision-making process.

- Being comfortable with a new system can also lead to innovation. As end users explore and utilize its capabilities, this can result in the improvement of various processes.

- Adopting end users promotes a culture of growth and learning within an organization. It encourages them to develop new skills and adopt new processes and technologies, which can foster a continuous learning environment.

End-user adoption goes beyond merely getting them to use a new technology. It involves making sure that the system performs to its full capabilities and leads to beneficial outcomes for both the users and the company. This is a crucial aspect of any process or system implementation, and it should be considered in any strategy.

How to Improve User Adoption?

To successfully implement new technology, process, or systems, end-user adoption has to be improved. There are various strategies that can help:

- One of the most important factors that can be considered when it comes to improving the end-user adoption of a new system is providing comprehensive training. This can be done in the form of online tutorials, in-person sessions, or workshops.

- Another important factor that can be considered when it comes to implementing a new system is communication. This will help the end users understand the benefits of the new system.

- Involve the users in the process of selection or implementation. Doing so can make them feel valued, and this can help them become more willing to adopt a new system.

- Support and guidance should be provided continuously to the users. This can be done by a dedicated support team or a help desk.

- A feedback mechanism should be established so that end users can share their suggestions, challenges, and experiences. This will not only help with the system's improvement, but it will also make them feel valued.

- When implementing a new system, consider doing it gradually instead of a complete overhaul. This will allow the users to get used to the new system without getting overwhelmed.

- Rewarding and recognizing the end users who quickly adopt a new system and use it efficiently will motivate others to do the same.

The goal is to make sure that the end users are using the new system efficiently and effectively. This involves continuous engagement from both the users and the management team.

Driving User Adoption and Engagement with Viva Engage

Getting the most out of your technology investments can be daunting, especially when it comes to implementing new technology. This section of the book will help you navigate through the various steps in the process of adopting Microsoft Viva Engage among employees at all levels of the organization. It will also help you to ensure that your employees are well equipped with the necessary skills and knowledge for a successful adoption. Table 2-1 shows the adoption strategy for Viva Engage.

Table 2-1. *Five Steps of Viva Engage Adoption Framework*

Step	Description
Strategy	Develop strategic business goals and involve organization stakeholders
Assessment	Identify AS-IS and TO-BE stages by doing gap analysis
Implementation	Roll out Viva Engage with a company-wide announcement
Training and Comms	Provide training and publish regular communication
Value Generation	Define metrics to measure business values such as North Start metric

Strategy:

After defining organizational business goals, link them closely with Viva Engage Adoption in such a way that Viva Engage will help in achieving these goals. Business goals linked to Viva Engage could be as follows:

- What are the top three business priorities of the organization and how will Viva Engage help them facilitate?

- What are the core values of the organization and how will Viva Engage help them to nurture them among employees?

- How will Viva Engage help organizations to work like a network and build knowledge communities?

Further, to adopt new technology, you need the support and buy-in from all parts of the organization. The following individuals can help you bridge the gap between technology and business outcomes. Before the rollout can be successful, both the HR and IT departments will have to work together to align the employee experience and technical scenarios.

- **Management Sponsors**: The Viva Engage vision and values should be communicated to all employees and the organization's leaders. Also, there must be regular interactions between IT and HR departments to identify and prioritize the needs of the organization where Viva Engage can be successfully adopted. Reinforce the adoption of the platform by actively participating in its operations.

- **Success Managers**: Ensure that business goals are closely linked to the adoption of Viva Engage.

- **Program Managers**: Oversee the Viva Engage rollout.

- **Superusers**: Onboard communities and be the first point of contact for all user queries.

- **Trainers**: Train early adopters and publish training-related content.

- **Stakeholders**: From each department Stakeholders will be identified and they will decide on how to use Viva Engage in their respective departments.

- **IT Teams**: Manage technical aspects of Viva Engage such as administrative privileges and involve Viva Engage in the technology road map of the organization.

- **Internal Comms Leads**: Manage company-wide Viva Engage communication.

- **HR Managers**: Fit Viva Engage into the employee ecosystem. Inform Viva Engage rollout timelines to the organization.

- **Community Managers**: Manage day-to-day user operations to build communities.

Assessment

Before you implement Viva Engage, it's important that you have the necessary infrastructure and people in place to support it. This will allow you to make informed decisions and improve the efficiency of your organization. One of the most important factors that you should consider is the readiness of your users.

The ability to determine the readiness of an organization and the appetite of its users for change requires a clear understanding of the organization's vision and the amount of change required. It is important that you thoroughly analyze the previous rollouts and identify the factors that contributed to its success. You should also consider the various factors that will affect the rollout, such as the availability of training and other resources.

Identify the individuals who will be most affected by the changes. This will allow you to create a collaboration space that will allow them to share their experiences and best practices. For instance, the early adopters might not be used to interacting with other people. You should also look at the various investments that your organization has made in social media and other related platforms. For instance, does your company subscribe to any of the social media platforms such as Facebook, First Up, or Jive? You should determine how you can use these platforms to improve the efficiency of your organization.

Employee experience and community engagement should be examined across the organization. This can be done by asking yourself if your staff members are dedicating enough time to social media and community content and if they're contributing to the culture of the company. Many organizations fail to utilize other solutions and investments due to the lack of engagement beyond the departmental silos and team members. A community-oriented organization creates connection and communication within its walls.

Implementation

Leverage resources such as Setting up Viva Engage License, configure review and privacy policies, and install Viva Engage in Microsoft Teams, which can be done during the initial part of the implementation as shown in Figure 2-1.

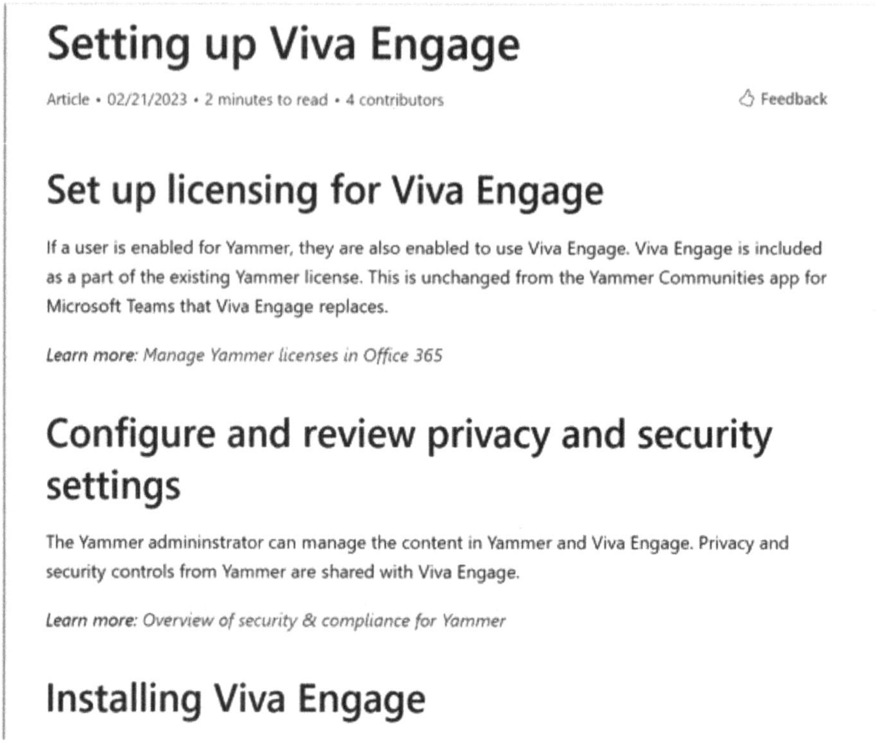

Setting up Viva Engage

Article • 02/21/2023 • 2 minutes to read • 4 contributors   ♢ Feedback

Set up licensing for Viva Engage

If a user is enabled for Yammer, they are also enabled to use Viva Engage. Viva Engage is included as a part of the existing Yammer license. This is unchanged from the Yammer Communities app for Microsoft Teams that Viva Engage replaces.

Learn more: Manage Yammer licenses in Office 365

Configure and review privacy and security settings

The Yammer admininstrator can manage the content in Yammer and Viva Engage. Privacy and security controls from Yammer are shared with Viva Engage.

Learn more: Overview of security & compliance for Yammer

Installing Viva Engage

Figure 2-1. *Deployment settings for Viva Engage*

Kick-start using Viva Engage for your coworkers and leaders to connect with one another and share their personal stories and questions. It combines the power of social networking platform Yammer with new capabilities that allow individuals to share their own stories and experiences. Through Viva Engage communities, your employees can connect with one another based on their interests, experiences, and roles. It gives them a sense of belonging and helps you shape and expand your culture. Leaders can use this platform to connect with their employees and inspire them to reach their goals. Employees also want to participate in the company's mission and clarity of purpose.

People can ask questions, share ideas, and exchange knowledge using Viva Engage. It enables organizations to connect with individuals across different business units and working groups, harnessing the power of diverse perspectives and experiences to solve problems and accelerate innovation. Employees can be activated to add their expertise and experience, and when they feel included, they are more inclined to contribute.

Training and Communication

Get your team organized and ready for the launch with a plan that includes key dates, training sessions, and materials. This will include the following:

- Create network awareness.

- Demonstrate support for network goals.

- Support community leadership.

- Drive engagement and adoption.

- Train on how to use Viva Engage.

Make Viva Engage the hub for your company's activities and communities by sharing what's happening in the organization. You can also launch a campaign or an Ask Me Anything event to encourage your team to participate in the conversation. Leaders should encourage their subordinates to ask for challenges and feedback, such as the one that a customer recently hosted. They can also log on to the platform weekly to respond or react to the conversations. Champion your conversations and celebrate wins big and small.

A training strategy may include that your employees are aware of the reasons behind Viva Engage. This includes the benefits it offers, how it can help them connect with others, and what it is all about. Using real-life work scenarios can help your audience members learn how to use technology. You can also ask champions to help develop scenarios for their local communities.

Training sessions should be conducted in multiple formats to accommodate various learning styles and geographical limitations. Make sure that the training continues to be reinforced with various options, such as on-demand training or lunch-and-learn sessions.

A communication plan will include a teaser campaign, first-day adoption event, launch campaigns, and tips campaigns. A teaser campaign will include an email or Viva Engage announcement about its business value and publish what's in for employees. Publish user guides and help articles on the first-day adoption event. Launch campaigns may include a Viva Engage screensaver across company devices and animation at the company reception office. Finally, tips campaigns will cover assistance to superusers of Viva Engage to build and drive efficient collaboration with communities.

Value Generation

To see value in Viva Engage, with the Microsoft 365 admin center, you can easily monitor and analyze the adoption of your products and improve the learning experience of your organization. This includes reports and analytics that can be used to identify areas of focus and improve the effectiveness of your leadership.

Comprehending the sentiments of users about Viva Engage through a survey can provide you with valuable insight into the program's success. Before you start using Viva Engage, conduct a survey to gather information about the users' experiences. After about halfway through the program's launch, conduct another survey to gather data about the users' experiences. Then, release the final survey 90 days following the launch. This will help you measure the program's effectiveness and improve the productivity and satisfaction of your users.

One of the most critical factors that businesses consider when it comes to value generation is cultural change. This can be done through the development of new training and examples that are designed to help employees connect with the tools. We can also encourage employees to use the tools by sharing success stories and learning about the multiple features of Microsoft Viva Engage.

Viva Engage Adoption Best Practices

The following are some best practices around user adoption that will assist anyone who intends to actively participate in the adoption of Viva Engage across the organization:

- You must understand the ins and outs of configuring Viva Engage to effectively serve your organization's needs. This guide will give you an overview of the necessary steps to implement the platform.

- Employees should be given a specific date when they can start using Viva Engage, which is typically tied to an organizational change or an announcement.

- Before you start implementing Viva Engage, you should first test it with a pilot group. Then, gather feedback to help shape the platform's launch.

- Before you start using Viva Engage, it's important that you introduce your employees to the various features and scenarios that can help them solve their problems.

- Throughout the rollout, you can also empower and leverage your champions. You can modify the plan based on their feedback.

- Set up groups and encourage leaders to respond and post content. Also, encourage them to use mobile apps or send messages through Outlook.

In the section, we will focus our best practices on leadership adoption, the use of All Company community as an internal communication channel, and the use of Viva Engage from Teams, mobile, or Outlook.

Leadership Adoption

Through Viva Engage, leaders can improve their communication efforts and establish a more effective relationship with their employees. It can facilitate two-way conversations between workers and managers, and it can drive discussions across the organization using various tools, such as town halls and Q&As. Leaders can share uplifting moments from your day-to-day activities. Post photos of your team and celebrate achievements, milestones, and promotions. Moreover, share news about your company and products. Further from creating a weekly top-of-mind video, record a clip that features a link to a podcast or article that you've been listening to or reading.

The following are some ways where leadership teams can remain engaged with Viva Engage:

- Schedule an Ask Me Anything event.

- Encourage leaders to share conversations and photos from their customers' meetings and events.

- Create a poll due to audience help.

- Use announcement to publish updates such as policy changes, organization restructure, and others.

- Use Viva Engage live events to broadcast events on major organizational topics.

- Set delegation for posting if the executives are busy.

- Leaders using the @mention feature to pull other leaders into the conversation.

- Encourage leaders to use the Viva Engage storyline feature.

- Further, encourage leaders to use the like, comment, or share feature to an existing conversation.

- Finally, leaders must encourage the use of Viva Engage mobile app.

By using the preceding approach, leadership teams can remain engaged on the Viva Engage platform and inspire others to be part of it.

Use of All Company As an Internal Communication Channel

All Company is a default community in Viva Engage once users sign in to it. The conversation from the All Company community is visible to all users of the Viva Engage; hence, it creates an opportunity to use this community as a strategic communication channel for all internal communication. The following are some ways in which the All Company community can be used as a strategic communication channel for internal communication:

- Add a description, cover picture, and icon for the All Company community.

- Delete roles such as leaders, admins, and corporate communicators.

- Describe its objectives and community guidelines.

- Host town halls in this All Company community.

- Encourage employees to use "All Company" Community for conversations related to all employees.

- Manage user access to post in All Company.

- Seed some initial content in All Company for user engagement.

Interact with Viva Engage from Teams, Mobile, or Email

Pin Viva Engage in Microsoft Teams and download the mobile app, respond to Viva Engage conversations from Outlook, and adjust email notifications as shown in Figure 2-2.

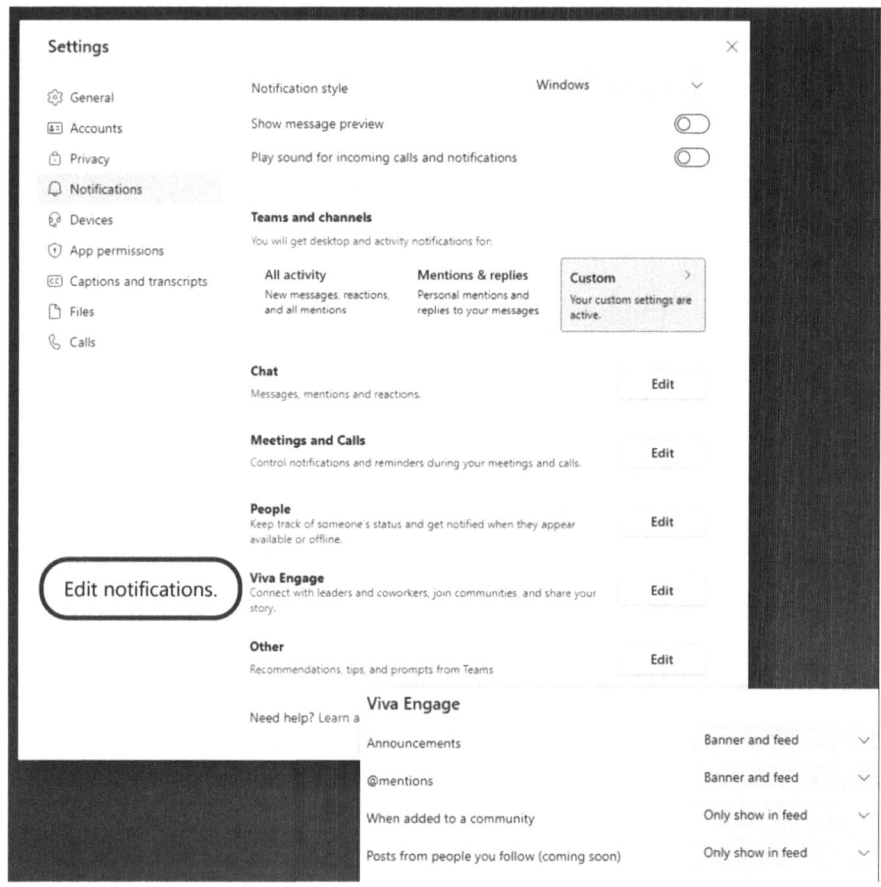

Figure 2-2. *Configure Viva Engage in MS Teams*

Best practices around leadership adoption, the use of All Company community as an internal communication channel, and the use of Viva Engage from Teams, mobile, or Outlook will assist community managers and all Viva Engage users to create engagement and deliver value.

Summary

With this, we have come to the end of this chapter on strategies to adopt user adoption using Viva Engage. This chapter introduced the reader to the concept of user adoption, as well as the various steps involved in implementing it. It also covered the ways in which Viva Engage user adoption can be achieved across all levels of organizational hierarchy. In addition, it provided a variety of Viva Engage training and communication plans that can be utilized by employees. Finally, it offered guidance on the creation and nurturing of communities. In the next chapter, we will learn how Viva Engage can be leveraged to foster engagement between leaders and employees, which will cover topics such as leadership engagement techniques in Viva Engage, metrics to measure the effectiveness of leadership engagement, benefits of leadership engagement in Viva Engage, and challenges in leadership engagement.

CHAPTER 3

Leadership Engagement: Empowering Leaders with Viva Engage

In the previous chapter, we have gained experience in understanding fundamentals of user adoption needs, benefits, and its implementation and driving user adoption with Viva Engage among employees at all levels of the organization, including communication plans, training programs, and incentivization approaches. Finally, we have gained experience around the creation and nurturing of communities within Viva Engage. The goal of this chapter is to understand how Viva Engage can be leveraged to foster engagement between leaders and employees, which will cover topics such as leadership engagement techniques in Viva Engage, metrics to measure the effectiveness of leadership engagement, benefits of leadership engagement in Viva Engage, and challenges in leadership engagement.

© The Editor(s) (if applicable) and The Author(s),
under exclusive license to APress Media, LLC, part of Springer Nature 2024
C. Waghmare, *Engage, Excel, and Elevate with Microsoft Viva Engage*, Apress Pocket Guides,
https://doi.org/10.1007/979-8-8688-0766-4_3

Introduction

Viva Engage is a platform that enables leaders to foster a culture that values innovation, transparency, and trust. When they actively participate, they can set an example for others by demonstrating how valuable collaboration and open communication are. By actively participating in the communication process, leaders can bridge the gap between themselves and their employees and ensure that the messages and objectives of the organization are clearly communicated. Transparency helps employees feel more informed about the decisions and actions of the organization, and it lowers the spread of false information. By sharing their personal stories and insights, leaders can become more relatable and approachable, which can help break down social hierarchies and foster a sense of belonging and community.

Being engaged and motivated by leaders can help boost employee morale and satisfaction. In addition to regular recognition, publicly celebrating the achievements of team members and individuals can also create a positive feedback loop that encourages employees to work harder. Further, being acknowledged and rewarded for the hard work that team members perform can help create a culture of appreciation. It can also help boost employee loyalty and retention. Moreover, by listening to and responding to the feedback of team members, leaders can improve the overall job satisfaction of their employees.

Through Viva Engage, leaders can promote professional development and knowledge sharing. This can be beneficial for employees as it allows them to receive mentorship and guidance from experienced leaders. It can also help them develop their talents and improve their performance. Providing a variety of learning resources and promoting professional development through the platform can help reinforce the company's commitment to skill and learning.

Leaders can influence the development and implementation of new processes and strategies. They can help employees understand the advantages of such changes and overcome their resistance by championing them. An encouraging culture of innovation, which encourages workers to collaborate and share their ideas, can result in new and innovative approaches that can help companies gain a competitive advantage. Leadership engagement can help develop this mindset by offering encouragement and recognition for experimentation and creative thinking.

Leadership engagement can also help organizations align their goals with the company's culture. It ensures that all employees are aware of the organization's objectives and vision, leading to a unified and synchronized effort across the firm. This alignment is vital for maintaining a competitive edge and attaining long-term success.

By being active in Viva Engage, leaders can improve responsiveness and decision-making within their organizations. By constantly interacting with their staff members and understanding their concerns, they can make better decisions that are geared toward the needs of the company. This responsiveness can also help in addressing issues that are affecting the organization, such as the timely resolution of problems. It promotes a sense of empowerment and inclusion.

Being active in leadership can help build a resilient and adaptable organization. During times of crisis or change, leaders can provide their staff members with supportive and transparent communication, which can help keep them focused and informed. This type of communication is very important to maintaining a positive work environment. Encouraging workers to embrace change and promoting adaptability can help companies remain agile and take advantage of new opportunities.

Being active in leadership can also help develop a culture that is conducive to the success of the organization. Through Viva Engage, leaders can promote various cultural programs, such as inclusion and diversity initiatives. They can show their commitment to making the organization more inclusive by participating in these kinds of projects. Being active in Viva Engage can also help develop a culture that is conducive to the success of the company. It can reinforce the organization's principles and values, which can create a work environment that is enjoyable and full of respect and admiration for one's peers.

Viva Engage engagement can help boost the organization's employer brand and reputation. Fostering a supportive and transparent atmosphere attracts and retains top talent, and leaders can exhibit their dedication and commitment to the well-being of their employees to make the organization an industry leader.

Being active in leadership in Viva Engage can help develop an organization's culture and make it more inclusive. It can boost employee morale, encourage professional growth, and align the strategic alignment of the company. By actively participating in the platform, leaders can make their workforce more resilient, motivated, and engaged, ultimately leading to a long-term success. By consistently and meaningfully engaging with Viva Engage, leaders can elevate the platform to a powerful tool that can facilitate innovation, organizational progress, and collaboration.

Leadership Engagement Techniques in Viva Engage

Viva Engage's leadership capabilities can help organizations foster a culture of innovation and productivity. Through effective techniques, leaders can transform the platform into a dynamic tool that enables them to connect with their constituents and drive innovation. This section will cover the various steps that leaders can take to improve their effectiveness on the platform.

Establishing a Strong Presence

- A professional and complete profile is very important for leaders to build credibility and attract potential customers. It should include a photo, their bio, and contact details. Besides their professional and personal information, profiles should also include details about their interests and role.

- Leaders must regularly log in to Viva Engage to maintain their visibility and keep in touch with their employees. This approach can help build trust and keep workers engaged.

- To make their communication more personal, leaders should regularly address their employees using their names. They should also acknowledge their contributions and respond to their comments in a personal manner. This approach shows that they value their workers and recognize their contributions.

Effective Content Sharing

- Leaders should regularly update their employees about the company's goals, progress, and initiatives. This ensures that workers stay informed and can keep up with the organization's direction. Open communication about successes and challenges fosters a culture of trust.

- Sharing thought leadership material, including articles, industry trends, and insights, positions executives as knowledgeable and encouraging employees to think critically and creatively.

- They should also use various forms of media, such as videos, podcasts, and infographics, to maintain a dynamic and engaging dialogue. Compared to text, multimedia content is more effective at conveying information.

Encouraging Participation and Collaboration

- Post interactive polls, surveys, and questions to encourage employees to interact. These posts can help workers share their thoughts and ideas, which can foster a sense of ownership and involvement. For instance, conducting a poll on the town hall topics that will be discussed in the next meeting can help boost engagement.

- In Viva Engage, let everyone know about the contributions of their employees. In addition to recognizing individual achievements, leaders can also highlight team accomplishments and fresh ideas to keep the workforce motivated.

- They should participate in and initiate open forums on various subjects. By engaging in discussions about organizational changes, industry trends, and feedback from staff members, leaders can foster a more collaborative and inclusive atmosphere.

Facilitating Knowledge Sharing

- In Viva Engage, leaders can create and manage resource libraries, which can contain training materials, reference guides, and documents. These can help employees find and use information easily.

- Leaders can connect with their employees through regular Q&A sessions and webinars. These events can be used to discuss topics such as industry insights, tips on professional development, and updates from the company. By hosting these events, leaders are demonstrating their commitment to employee engagement.

- Leaders can create and manage forums and panels on certain topics, and they can invite experts to share their insights and knowledge in order to provide employees with valuable experiences.

Promoting a Culture of Innovation

- In Viva Engage, leaders can host hackathons and innovation challenges, which encourage staff members to come up with novel ideas to solve problems at work. Such events can help promote a culture of creativity and continuous improvement.

- Virtual idea incubators are tools that allow employees to share their ideas and collaborate. This approach enables leaders to provide feedback and support, which would help turn their suggestions into viable projects. It also empowers workers to be part of the company's innovation efforts.

- Leaders should encourage their subordinates to experiment and take risks. Providing a safe environment where workers can learn from failures and try new approaches can foster a more innovative mindset.

Building Community and Culture

- Through cultural programs, leaders can promote their organizations' diversity and inclusion initiatives. They can also participate in various wellness activities and community projects. By backing these programs through Viva Engage, they show their commitment to fostering an inclusive and positive culture.

- Organizations can celebrate various achievements and milestones, such as the completion of a project or an anniversary, which can boost morale and encourage a sense of community and cooperation. Such celebrations should be shared with the entire organization through Viva Engage.

- By sharing stories about the past, present, and future of their organizations, leaders can help strengthen the bonds of trust and cooperation among their constituents. Moreover, they can use storytelling to promote the company's culture, inspire individuals, and celebrate the achievements of their enterprise.

Supporting Employee Well-Being and Development

- In Viva Engage, leaders can promote their well-being initiatives and programs. By sharing tips on how to manage stress, stay healthy, and balance their work and personal lives, they can encourage their employees to prioritize their well-being.

- They can promote and establish mentorship programs, which can help develop the skills of emerging talent and facilitate career advancement. By working with experienced individuals, companies can help promote knowledge transfer. Leaders can leverage Viva Engage to endorse and highlight these connections.

- They should publicize information about professional development and learning opportunities. Listing training sessions, workshops, and courses can encourage individuals to continue improving their skills.

Enhancing Feedback Loops

- Through regular polls and surveys in Viva Engage, leaders can get a better understanding of their employees' opinions and improve the organization's performance. These tools can also help them identify areas of improvement and gather feedback on their initiatives.

- To ensure that their employees feel safe and supported, leaders should establish effective feedback platforms that encourage them to share their thoughts. They can also show that they care about their employees' feedback by taking action whenever necessary.

- Follow-up is necessary. Leaders should regularly provide updates on the actions they've taken based on feedback. Doing so shows that they value their employees' contributions and commitment to continuous improvement.

Aligning with Organizational Goals

- Viva Engage can help leaders align their teams with the company's objectives. By regularly sharing the organization's vision and mission, leaders can make sure that all members are working toward the same goals.

- By regularly sharing information about their initiatives' progress, leaders can keep their team members motivated and informed. They can also celebrate achievements and address concerns in a transparent manner.

- Viva Engage's leaders should interact with both internal and external clients and stakeholders. By facilitating open communication with partners, associates, and clients, leaders can cultivate stronger bonds and enhance the firm's reputation.

Leveraging Technology and Analytics

- With the help of Viva Engage's analytics features, leaders can monitor employee sentiment, track engagement levels, and analyze trends. By analyzing this data, they can make informed decisions regarding how to improve the effectiveness of their organizations.

- Viva Engage can be further enhanced by integrating with other Microsoft 365 platforms and tools. This can involve working with offerings such as OneDrive, Microsoft Teams, and SharePoint. This will help improve the efficiency of their organizations' workflows.

- It is important for leaders to keep up with the latest changes in Viva Engage so that they can create and implement effective strategies for their organizations.

Long-Term Sustainability and Impact

- A long-term strategy for Viva Engage should be established by leaders. It should include goals, milestones, and methods for sustaining engagement.

- Viva Engage's effectiveness depends on a team effort. This is why leaders must establish a group of individuals who can help with the platform administration, content creation, and interaction support.

- They should also regularly celebrate the achievements of Viva Engage to maintain motivation and momentum. In addition, leaders should talk about how the platform has helped boost employee engagement and company objectives.

Overcoming Challenges

- Due to the limited time that leaders have available to engage with Viva Engage, they often find themselves unable to complete all of their tasks. To help manage their workload, leaders can schedule time for dedicated activities and delegate tasks to their team members.

- Leaders may feel hesitant about using Viva Engage
  due to their resistance to its features. By providing
  training and exhibiting its value, leaders can overcome
  this obstacle. They should also share their own best
  practices and stories to show how engagement can
  positively affect their organizations.

- Being consistent in your engagement is often a
  challenge. To help keep it in check, leaders should set
  goals and create a content calendar. They should also
  regularly review and adjust their engagement strategy.

Finally, leaders must be engaged in Viva Engage to foster a culture
of innovation and productivity. They can take advantage of various
techniques to improve their profiles, promote well-being, and encourage
participation. To overcome obstacles such as resistance and time
constraints, leaders must adopt a committed and strategic approach.
By actively participating in Viva Engage, leaders can improve their
communication skills, align their organizations' strategic goals, and foster
a stronger community among their staff. By integrating the platform
with other Microsoft 365 tools, they can create a more collaborative and
dynamic work environment that can help sustain the company's success.
Consistent and thoughtful engagement can help transform Viva Engage
into an asset for employee engagement and organizational growth.

**Some practical application of Viva Engage leadership engagement
techniques:**

The leadership team of a financial services company can use Viva
Engage to promote innovation and strategic alignment. The company's
managers can keep their employees informed about market trends and
regulatory changes, as well as their priorities, through regular updates. They
can also organize challenges to foster fresh thinking. The company's CEO
participates in the challenges, giving feedback and identifying the best ideas.
This active involvement promotes continuous improvement and innovation.

The leadership team of a healthcare organization can use Viva Engage to promote professional development and wellness for its employees. The organization's managers can regularly share resources related to work-life balance, stress management, and health tips. They can also encourage training and educational opportunities, such as conferences. The company's Chief Marketing Officer holds monthly Q&A sessions about Viva Engage to discuss employee concerns and share industry news. This approach to development and wellness helps boost employee retention and satisfaction.

The founders of a tech startup can use Viva Engage to establish a culture of trust and support. They talk about their company's journey, celebrate achievements, and honor employees. The platform can also be used to promote inclusion and diversity initiatives, which encourage workers to share their experiences and participate in discussions. The founders can help employees feel valued and inspired to contribute to the success of the company.

Metrics to Measure Leadership Engagement in Viva Engage

The goal of assessing leadership effectiveness in Viva Engage is to identify areas of concern that leaders can improve and make a difference in the company's culture. There are a variety of metrics that can be used to measure this type of engagement, and they can be categorized into qualitative and quantitative categories. In this section, we will talk about a framework that will allow you to evaluate the multiple aspects of leadership on the platform as shown in Table 3-1.

Table 3-1. *Leadership Engagement Metrics*

Quantitative Analytics	Qualitative Analytics	Advanced Analytical Techniques
Activity Metrics • Number of Posts • Frequency of Posts • Number of Comments • Likes and Reactions • Shares	Sentiment Analysis • Sentiment of Comments • Tone of Communication	Natural Language Processing (NLP) • NLP Techniques • Topic Modeling
Engagement Metrics • Employee Engagement • Engagement Rate • Response Time	Content Quality • Relevance and Value • Variety of Content	Social Network Analysis (SNA) • SNA Analysis • Centrality Measure
Reach and Impact Metrics • Reach • Impressions • Engagement Spread	Employee Feedback • Surveys and Polls • Focus Groups	Engagement Segmentation • Segment Engagement • Engagement Heatmaps
Network Metrics • Connections • Interaction Network	Impact on Organizational Culture • Cultural Alignment • Behavioral Changes	

Quantitative Metrics

- **Activity Metrics**

  - **Number of Posts**: The goal of this metric is to measure the total number of posts that leaders made over a specific period. It allows one to evaluate their level of engagement in initiating and sharing content.

  - **Frequency of Posts**: Leaders can measure their Viva Engage activity by looking at how frequently they post. Regular engagement is an indication of their commitment to the platform and their continuous presence.

  - **Number of Comments**: The number of comments that leaders make on their posts is measured based on their responsiveness and willingness to participate in discussions that others initiate.

  - **Likes and Reactions**: Leaders can also monitor the reactions and likes that their posts receive. High levels of engagement can help determine if the content resonates with workers.

  - **Shares**: The number of times that leaders' posts are shared by other individuals can be tracked to determine their relevance and value.

- **Engagement Metrics**

  - **Employee Engagement**: The goal of this measure is to analyze the level of engagement of staff members with regard to the posts of leaders. It involves metrics such as likes, shares, and comments.

- **Engagement Rate:** The total number of likes, shares, and comments divided by the number of posts will determine the engagement rate.

- **Response Time:** This metric will give you an idea of the average level of engagement. Leaders should be aware of the average time it takes them to respond to questions and comments. A quick response time indicates active engagement and good communication.

- **Reach and Impact Metrics**

  - **Reach:** The number of unique workers who have viewed the posts of leaders should be measured. High reach indicates that the messages of the leaders are being widely perceived throughout the organization.

  - **Impressions:** The count of times leaders' posts have been viewed is used to measure the level of visibility of their content on the platform.

  - **Engagement Spread:** The distribution of engagement across various departments and locations can be analyzed to determine if the posts are reaching a wider audience or if they are being concentrated in a particular area.

- **Network Metrics**

  - **Connections:** Analyzing the number of followers or connections of leaders in Viva Engage can help you determine if they are connected to the organization. Many of these connections suggest that they are easily accessible.

- **Interaction Network**: The structure and density of the interactions between workers and leaders can be visualized by mapping the network. This approach can also highlight patterns and influencers.

Qualitative Metrics

- **Sentiment Analysis**

  - **Sentiment of Comments**: The sentiment of comments made on the social media posts of leaders can be analyzed to gauge their employees' feelings. Positive feedback indicates that their messages are received well, while negative feedback can highlight areas of concern.

  - **Tone of Communication**: Evaluate the tone of the comments and posts made by leaders. A more encouraging or supportive tone can foster a more positive work environment, while a more distant or formal tone can negatively affect engagement.

- **Content Quality**

  - **Relevance and Value**: Leaders should determine the value and relevance of their posts. High-quality content should appeal to workers' interests and needs, and it can inspire engagement.

  - **Variety of Content**: Evaluate the various types of content utilized by leaders, such as polls, infographics, text posts, and videos. Varying content can keep people engaged while catering to varying preferences.

- **Employee Feedback**

  - **Surveys and Polls**: To gauge the level of engagement, regular polls and surveys can be conducted to gather feedback from staff members about Viva Engage.

  - **Focus Groups**: To get a deeper understanding of how leaders are engaging with their staff, organize focus groups. These sessions can provide employees with an opportunity to share their experiences.

- **Impact on Organizational Culture**

  - **Cultural Alignment**: The level of engagement of leaders in Viva Engage can be assessed based on their alignment with the company's culture and values. The consistency of communication between leaders and the organization fosters cultural practices.

  - **Behavioral Changes**: Positive changes can be observed in the behavior of workers because of leadership. For instance, increased collaboration, staff participation in initiatives, and innovation can all be indicators of a favorable impact.

Advanced Analytical Techniques

- **Natural Language Processing (NLP)**

  - **NLP Technique**: Through this technique, you can analyze the posts and comments of leaders. This method can provide you with valuable insight into their topics and themes.

- **Topic Modeling**: By modeling the topics that leaders talk about, you can identify the trends that emerge in these discussions. This can help you understand the scope of their communication.

- **Social Network Analysis (SNA)**

  - **SNA Analysis**: Through SNA, you can gain a deeper understanding of how interactions in Viva Engage work. It will also identify the key influencers and clusters within the organization.

  - **Centrality Measure**: To determine the level of importance that a leader has to the organization's communication network, you can calculate the centrality measure.

- **Engagement Segmentation**

  - **Segment Engagement**: By segmenting engagement data by organizational and demographic attributes, such as department, role, location, and tenure, you can identify groups that may be less engaged with the communication of leaders.

  - **Engagement Heatmaps**: Heatmaps can help visualize the levels of engagement across various groups. This can help identify areas where the need for improvement in leadership is greatest.

Implementation Strategy of Leadership Engagement Metrics

The Viva Engage platform should have clear goals for measuring how engaged leaders are. These should be aligned with the organization's priorities and objectives. KPIs are essential for measuring the effectiveness of the Viva Engage platform. They should be designed to be relevant to the organization's culture and goals.

A robust data collection process should be established to gather qualitative and quantitative information from Viva Engage. This data should then be integrated with other systems, such as performance management and HR, to provide a more holistic view of the organization. Setting up an automatic reporting system for leadership will ensure that the information is timely and actionable.

Regularly reviewing the progress of the leadership team and monitoring the engagement metrics, you can use this data to adjust your strategies and improve your performance. One of the most effective ways to improve the effectiveness of your leadership team is by establishing feedback loops that allow leaders to receive feedback on their efforts.

Leaders should be provided with the necessary training to ensure they are able to effectively utilize Viva Engage. This may include methods for responding to feedback and communication. Leaders can be assisted by mentors and coaches in improving their engagement skills. In addition, experienced leaders can offer their insights to help others.

Acknowledge and reward leaders who are consistently engaged with Viva Engage. Doing so can motivate others to follow suit. Leaders can be rewarded for their continuous efforts and positive Viva Engage outcomes.

Conclusion

A comprehensive analysis of how leaders are engaging with Viva Engage can be achieved through a combination of qualitative and quantitative methods. It can also be done using advanced analytical tools and strategies. Organizations can monitor the various activities of their leaders and gain a deeper understanding of how they are influencing the platform. A sentiment analysis, an assessment of the quality of content, and employee feedback can provide a deeper understanding of how leadership can be improved. In addition, techniques such as segmentation and NLP can be used to analyze engagement.

A framework for measuring and improving leadership engagement needs to be in place, and it should include continuous monitoring and support for the leaders. Highlighting and rewarding effective efforts can motivate individuals to take part in Viva Engage and help foster a more collaborative and innovative culture.

Benefits of Leadership Engagement

Through the Viva Engage platform, leadership development can help organizations achieve their goals and improve their performance. It provides a framework for developing a culture of trust and transparency. By actively participating in Viva Engage, leaders can set an example for their employees by demonstrating that collaboration and dialogue are valued. This report will explore the various ways in which leadership engagement can transform a company.

One of the most important benefits of leadership development is the ability to improve communication across the organization. Through Viva Engage, leaders can regularly share their insights and goals, which can help employees stay informed about the company's progress. Transparency reduces rumors and uncertainties, making employees feel more secure and encouraging a more organized vision. By aligning all members of the organization with the company's goals, it can help drive collective success.

Being engaged by leaders can boost employee morale and satisfaction. They can also make their teams feel valued and supported, which can help them perform at their best. When leaders publicly recognize staff members for their achievements, it can help motivate them and encourage them to go beyond their duties. It can additionally foster a culture of respect and appreciation.

Viva Engage can help promote professional development and learning by allowing leaders to provide their staff members with mentorship and guidance. This can be particularly helpful for those who aspire to be high-performing employees. Leaders can foster a growth mindset among their staff members by providing them with opportunities to learn and develop their skills.

Being engaged in conversations helps build a more welcoming and diverse environment for employees. It also helps leaders develop a more understanding of themselves and their role. This interaction can break down various barriers and create an environment where staff members feel comfortable discussing their ideas. By fostering two-way communication, organizations can develop more innovative approaches and foster a more collaborative culture.

One of the most important benefits of being engaged in conversations is the ability to make more informed decisions. Through conversations with employees, leaders can gain a deeper understanding of their team's challenges and opportunities. This interaction can also help them improve their responsiveness and make informed decisions.

Leadership engagement through Viva Engage can result in higher levels of retention and employee loyalty. Viva Engage's data revealed that those who felt connected to their managers were more likely to be committed to the organization, and this resulted in improved performance, reduced turnover rates, and higher productivity. It also made them feel valued and heard.

Being engaged in conversations is very important during times of crisis or change. Leaders can help their team members manage their stress and keep them focused on their work by providing regular updates. This type of support can help them overcome the negative effects of change and uncertainty.

The organization's reputation can be improved by having a supportive and transparent leadership style. This type of style can help attract and retain top talent, and it can also help the company establish a positive work environment. By showing that it values its employees and is committed to creating a favorable work environment, the company can gain a competitive advantage.

Through Viva Engage, leaders can promote the culture and goals of the organization. They can reinforce the company's core values, mission, and vision by consistently communicating these values. This alignment of values and actions can help strengthen the company's overall culture and make all employees strive for the same objectives.

Viva Engage can help organizations drive change. Its leaders can use it to explain new initiatives and collect feedback, and it can help build a buy-in from the employees. This approach can also help decrease the resistance to change by making employees feel that their input was considered.

Viva Engage can help organizations foster innovation. By creating an environment that is inclusive and open, leaders can encourage staff members to collaborate and share their ideas, which can result in new approaches to problem-solving. Additionally, leaders can reward and recognize such ideas, which can encourage staff members to think critically and contribute to the company's success.

In summary, leadership engagement through Viva Engage can make a huge impact on an organization. It can help boost employee morale, cultivate a culture of continuous education, facilitate informed decision-making, and improve the company's reputation. In addition, it can help build an environment that encourages innovation and promote values. By fully participating in Viva Engage, leaders can make their organizations more dynamic and transparent, fostering a more collaborative, inclusive, and conducive to sustainability and long-term success. Viva Engage offers leaders an opportunity to amplify their organizations' vision and foster a more collaborative and positive culture.

Challenges in Leadership Engagement in Viva Engage

When it comes to using the Viva Engage platform, leaders face many challenges that can affect their ability to foster a collaborative environment, encourage open communication, and cultivate a positive work culture. To overcome these obstacles, they must first learn how to leverage the platform's capabilities while also addressing the unique features of its digital workspace. The following are some key issues that leaders encounter when using the platform.

Digital Fatigue

One of the most common issues that leaders face when using the Viva Engage platform is digital fatigue. This issue can affect their ability to retain and attract the attention of their employees. They often face an overwhelming amount of digital interactions, which can lead to burnout. They must make sure that their messages are engaging and concise. To effectively address this issue, leaders should prioritize the quality of their communications. They can also find creative ways to deliver their messages in order to prevent digital fatigue.

Building Authentic Connections

Establishing connections within a virtual space can be challenging, as it limits the ability of leaders to communicate their genuine intentions. They must be intentional about making their interactions more personal and showing concern for their staff members. By sharing personal stories, expressing vulnerability, and frequently acknowledging the efforts of their employees, leaders can bridge the gap.

Ensuring Consistent Engagement

It can be hard for busy executives to maintain consistent engagement in Viva Engage. It's because they must work full time and often have to answer comments, post updates, and participate in other discussions. To overcome these challenges, leaders should regularly integrate activities such as these into their daily routines. To avoid overburdening the leaders, delegating some tasks to team members can help keep the engagement routine consistent.

Navigating Diverse Communication Styles

A company has a diverse workforce that has varying styles and communication preferences. It can be hard for leaders to create effective messages that everyone will find engaging. They need to devise a strategy that includes the use of various forms of media, including video, interactive posts, and text, to cater to every individual's needs and ensure inclusivity.

Managing Resistance to Change

When it comes to implementing a new communication strategy, such as adopting new technologies, it can be hard for leaders and workers to come up with a common ground. They may also be uncomfortable with the platform's transparency requirements. To address this issue, leaders should train themselves on how to use the platform. They should also talk about how Viva Engage can help improve their company's collaboration and transparency.

Balancing Transparency and Confidentiality

While transparency is important for building trust and engaging with the public, leaders should also consider the delicate balance between maintaining confidentiality and being open. Disseminating too much information may expose sensitive data to unauthorized access, while keeping too little may result in a lack of trust and rumors, undermining public confidence. They must establish clear guidelines on how to share information in Viva Engage and make sure that all communications conform to the company's confidentiality rules. When it comes to maintaining credibility, leaders must strike a balance between discretion and openness.

Encouraging Active Participation

One of the biggest challenges that leaders face is encouraging their employees to actively participate. Even though they're doing their best to get the level of engagement up, it may still be low. This can be caused by a variety of factors, such as fear of being judged, disinterest, or uncertainty about the significance of taking part. To create an environment that's conducive to open discussion, leaders should establish a safe and welcoming atmosphere. They should reward and acknowledge participation, promote a culture of feedback, and show how their employees' input is valuable.

Integrating Viva Engage with Existing Workflows

Transitioning Viva Engage into the daily operations of an organization can be challenging. Since employees may perceive it as an additional tool rather than a significant enhancement to their work, leaders should work to demonstrate how it can help them improve their productivity and communication. They should also provide training on how to integrate the platform into their daily tasks, as well as highlight their own success stories.

Measuring the Impact of Engagement

Although some metrics can provide insight into the number of likes, comments, and posts in Viva Engage, they do not consider the impact that this type of activity has on employee morale, culture, and trust. To measure the effectiveness of this type of engagement, leaders should establish clear measurement frameworks. They should regularly conduct surveys and feedback loops to identify areas of their efforts where they can improve.

Maintaining Engagement Across Geographically Dispersed Teams

Being able to engage teams from different cultures and time zones can be a challenge for global organizations. Since they have to navigate various cultural differences and language barriers, leaders should regularly plan and conduct events that are convenient for everyone. They should also make sure that all members feel valued and understood by providing recordings for those who can't participate in live sessions.

Finally, while leadership in Viva Engage can be challenging, it can be managed effectively through a variety of strategies and methods. Some of these include developing a strategy that addresses digital fatigue, ensuring that the environment is inclusive, and addressing issues such as authenticity. By fostering intentional and thoughtful engagement, leaders can establish a connected and dynamic workplace that sparks achievement and promotes a sense of belonging and community among staff members.

With this, we have come to the end of this chapter. In this chapter, we have covered details on topics such as leadership engagement techniques in Viva Engage, metrics to measure the effectiveness of leadership engagement, benefits of leadership engagement in Viva Engage, and challenges in leadership engagement. In the upcoming chapter, we will discover how Viva Engage integrates with other Microsoft 365 tools and services, such as Microsoft Teams, SharePoint, and Yammer, to create a seamless digital workplace experience.

CHAPTER 4

Integration of Viva Engage with Microsoft 365

In the previous chapter, we have gained a good sense of understanding topics such as leadership engagement techniques in Viva Engage, metrics to measure the effectiveness of leadership engagement, benefits of leadership engagement in Viva Engage, and challenges in leadership engagement. In this chapter, we will explore how Viva Engage integrates with other Microsoft 365 tools and services, such as Microsoft Copilot, Teams, SharePoint, Outlook, and Power Automate to create a seamless digital workplace experience.

Effective collaboration and communication are crucial for organizations to succeed in today's digital world. With Microsoft Viva Engage, they can enhance their employee engagement and collaborate more effectively. It works seamlessly with Microsoft 365 services to create an ecosystem that promotes innovation and productivity. The various services that are included in Microsoft Viva Engage include Office 365, Copilot, Teams, SharePoint, Outlook, and Power Automate. This comprehensive overview explores how these services can help organizations create a unified digital workspace.

© The Editor(s) (if applicable) and The Author(s),
under exclusive license to APress Media, LLC, part of Springer Nature 2024
C. Waghmare, *Engage, Excel, and Elevate with Microsoft Viva Engage*, Apress Pocket Guides,
https://doi.org/10.1007/979-8-8688-0766-4_4

Copilot

With the help of AI, Microsoft Copilot can help users automate repetitive tasks and improve their content creation and sharing. It can also help them analyze and improve their engagement metrics. When integrated with Microsoft Viva Engage, it can provide suggestions and recommendations on topics that are relevant to their audience. AI-powered support enables employees to convey ideas in a more efficient and impactful manner, thereby improving the quality of their interactions.

With the help of Copilot in Viva Engage as shown in Figure 4-1, you can create and manage post recommendations and improve your online presence. You can also access the platform from anywhere you want, including your home feed, community, campaign, or storyline.

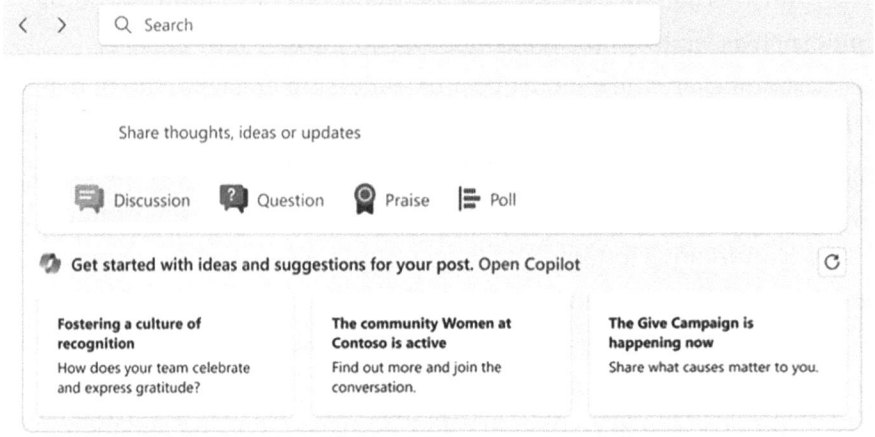

Figure 4-1. *Copilot in Viva Engage*

To expand the panel of recommendations in Viva Engage, select Show ideas as shown in Figure 4-2.

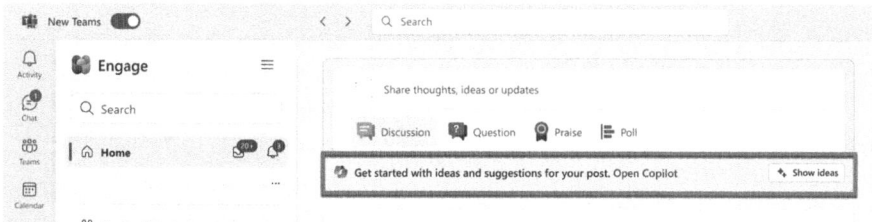

Figure 4-2. *Show ideas in Copilot*

After you've selected Open Copilot, a prompt will appear. You can then ask the platform for help. It will then suggest some prompts that will help you get started as shown in Figure 4-3.

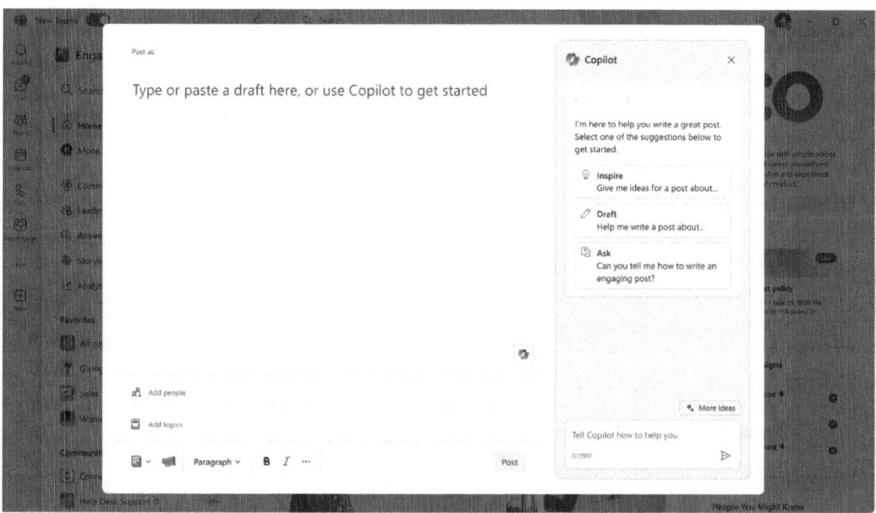

Figure 4-3. *Start chatting with Copilot in Viva Engage*

The prompt guide featured in the sparkle menu as in Figure 4-4 will help you work with Copilot in various ways, such as developing an engaging post and conveying what you want to say. It also offers examples of how you can ask the platform to give you feedback.

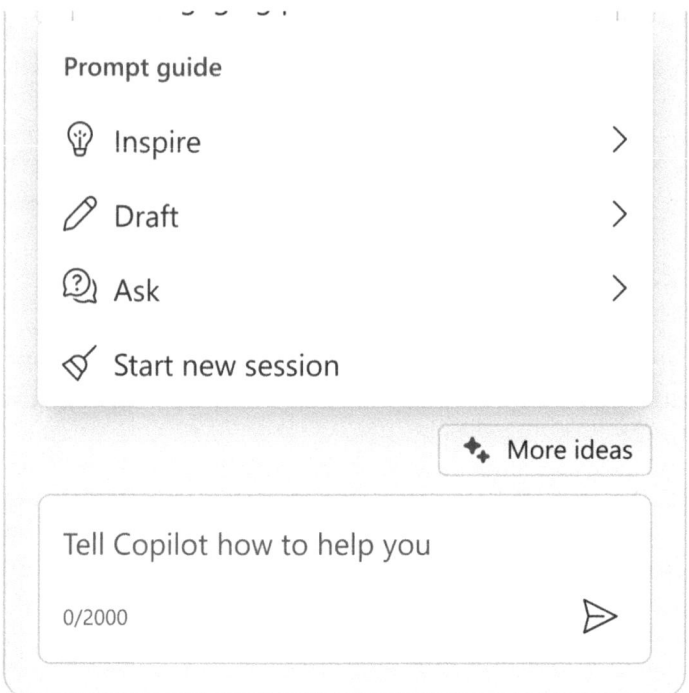

Figure 4-4. *Sparkle menu*

With Copilot in Viva Engage, you can easily access large language models with Microsoft's Responsible AI protections. There are many prompts that Copilot suggests that you can try out, but you can also come up with your own ideas for how to ask for help as shown in Figure 4-5. Throughout the journey, Copilot will help you cultivate a deeper understanding of yourself and your communication style.

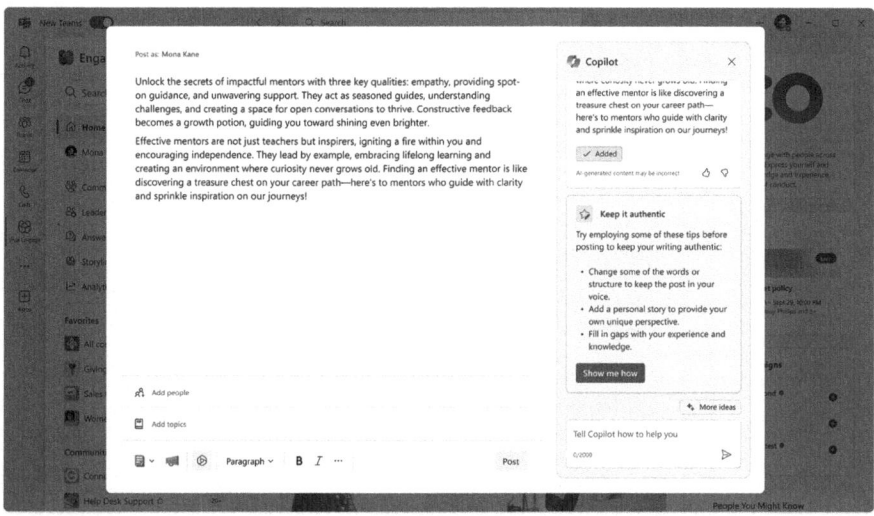

Figure 4-5. *Get creative with your new assistant*

From Figure 4-6, in Viva Engage, you can give feedback to the Copilot team whenever you use the tool. You can do so by clicking the "thumbs up" or "thumbs down" icon, and it will be reviewed regularly so that the team can identify areas of improvement.

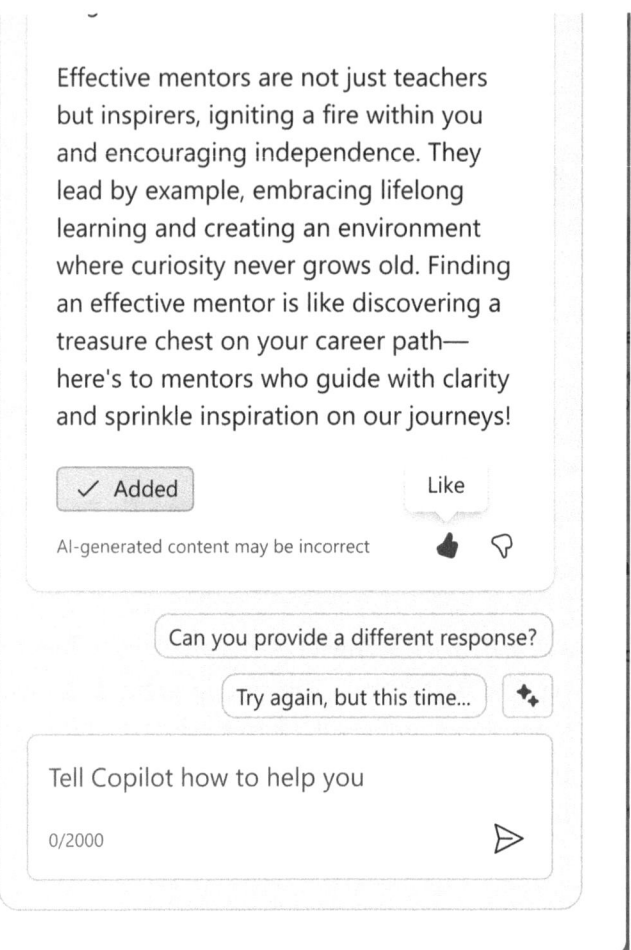

Figure 4-6. *Provide feedback about Copilot in Viva Engage*

With the help of large language model technology, Copilot in Viva Engage allows users to perform various tasks in a language like how they would ask a person. It learns from your interests and communities to identify areas where you can engage and post content that's relevant to you.

The Viva Engage and Copilot integration offers many advantages. Modern workplaces require effective collaboration and communication. The integration of Microsoft Copilot and Viva Engage, which brings together an AI-powered assistant and an employee engagement platform, provides companies with numerous advantages. The integration of Viva Engage and Copilot enables companies to improve the quality of their content and increase productivity. It also helps them automate various tasks and generate insights. Let's look at a few benefits as follows.

Enhanced Content Creation

One of the most important advantages of the integration of Viva Engage and Copilot is its ability to create engaging and high-quality content. With the help of AI, users can easily draft posts and generate responses to their questions. This feature can help employees keep track of important projects and meetings.

The integration of Copilot and Viva Engage enables employees to focus on their core responsibilities and tasks, resulting in reduced time spent creating content. Consistently crafted content utilizing Copilot's assistance ensures a well-defined and engaging tone throughout all communications, fostering a collaborative and positive culture.

Intelligent Insights and Analytics

One of the most significant advantages of the Viva Engage and Copilot integration is its ability to provide organizations with valuable analytics. Through the use of AI, Copilot's platform can analyze the various metrics of its users' engagement, such as likes, shares, and comments, to identify the most effective content for their campaigns. This feature can also help them identify which topics resonate with their employees and which ones generate the most engagement.

Communities and internal communication teams can benefit from this insight, as it allows them to develop their strategies based on the preferences and needs of their audience. For instance, if Copilot determines that posts about career advancement and training are popular, the company may want to create content related to such topics.

Automated Routine Tasks

Integrating Viva Engage and Copilot will enhance productivity by automating routine tasks. This includes handling tasks such as responding to frequent queries, maintaining community moderation, and posting updates. For instance, if an employee frequently asks about upcoming events or policies, Copilot can help them get answers immediately.

Not only does it reduce the time spent performing these tasks, but it also ensures that workers receive accurate and timely information. With the help of Copilot, employees can spend more time engaging in creative and strategic activities, which can boost their job satisfaction and productivity.

Improved Employee Engagement

The goal of Viva Engage is to create a sense of belonging and community among staff members. By integrating Copilot, this objective can be achieved by ensuring relevant and timely communication. The platform can help staff members stay engaged by suggesting topics for discussion, sharing popular posts, and motivating them to participate in ongoing discussions.

The ability of Copilot to provide recommendations based on an individual's past interactions and preferences can help boost engagement and connection. For example, if a staff member frequently interacts with content about wellness initiatives, Copilot can suggest related topics.

The integration of Copilot and Viva Engage can help enhance the content creation process and provide staff members with valuable insights. It can also help them improve their decision-making skills and increase their productivity. By AI, the two platforms can help organizations create a more collaborative and productive workplace. The integration of Viva Engage and Copilot can help organizations address the modern workplace's complex needs. It can help them create a more connected and productive environment.

Teams

The Microsoft Teams hub is designed to bring together people in Microsoft 365. With the integration of Viva Engage, users can easily participate in conversations and share updates within the Teams environment. The integration of Viva Engage will allow users to participate in more community activities, which will help promote open communication and foster a sense of belonging. Notifications from the app will also be displayed in Teams, allowing users to keep up with important updates.

If you're a Microsoft Teams user, you might want to add a tab that allows you to collaborate on topics and posts in the community. Your team members can then participate in the conversation and post their answers to the wider community. When a member of your team visits the Viva Engage tab, their authentication will be restored to ensure that they only see the content that they're authorized to see. You'll need to have a subscription to get started with Engage Enterprise. To add a tab, your team members must first be enabled. If they're not able to do so, contact your team owner. To add Viva Engage to a Teams channel:

- To select the + symbol, go to the Teams channel and click the tab bar. Refer to Figure 4-7a.

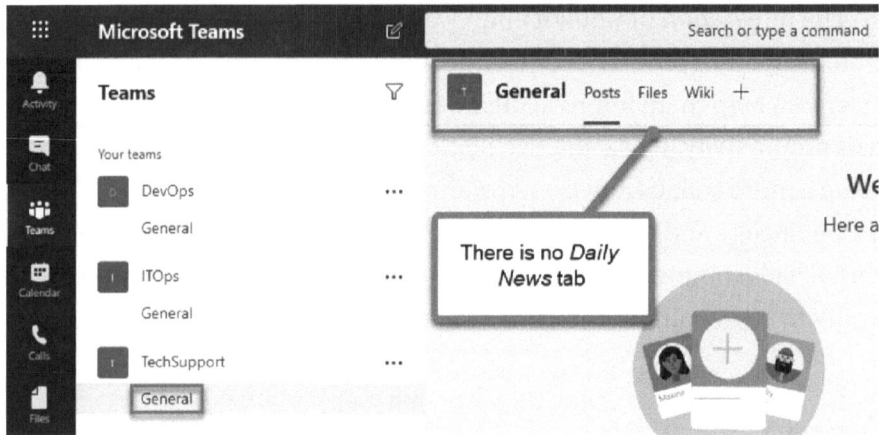

Figure 4-7a. *Click the "+" sign to add the Viva Engage app*

- Add the Viva Engage app from the list of apps as shown in Figure 4-7b.

Figure 4-7b. *Viva Engage app in the Teams app directory*

- To select a community, go to the search box and type the name of the community or topic that you want to include as shown in Figure 4-7c.

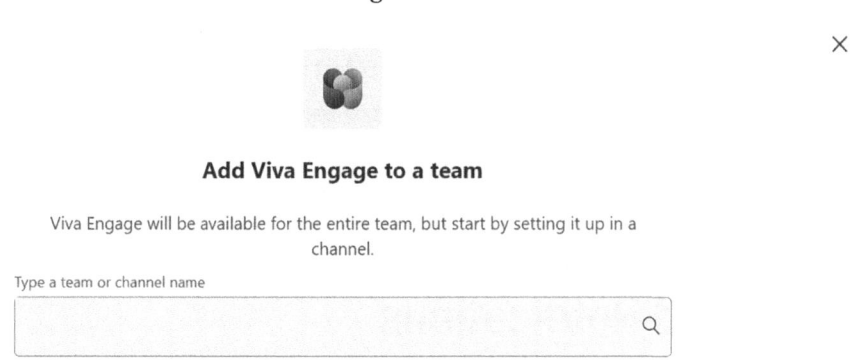

Add Viva Engage to a team

Viva Engage will be available for the entire team, but start by setting it up in a channel.

Type a team or channel name

Figure 4-7c. *Select a Viva Engage community to display messages in the Teams channel*

- To notify your team about the addition of the Viva Engage tab, ensure that the post to the channel has been selected. Otherwise, it should be clear.

- The new Viva Engage tab will be displayed in the team's Channel tab bar.

The benefits of integrating Microsoft Teams and Viva Engage are numerous. The integration of Viva Engage and Microsoft Teams can help organizations improve worker engagement and communication. It can also create a powerful toolset that enables productive and connected teams.

Seamless Communication

The integration of Viva Engage and Microsoft Teams enables employees to participate in social activities and collaborate on projects more effectively. It eliminates the need for them to switch between various applications and makes it easier for them to stay connected.

Enhanced Collaboration

Microsoft Teams is renowned for its robust collaboration tools, such as video meetings and file sharing. When incorporated with Viva Engage, these abilities can be further expanded to facilitate community interactions. For instance, staff members can initiate video calls or take advantage of the shared screens within a discussion, leading to more collaborative and dynamic teamwork.

Centralized Notifications

One of the most important advantages of the integration is the ability to send notifications to Microsoft Teams. This ensures that the company's employees are always aware of important updates and community activities. It helps keep them engaged and prevents them from missing vital information.

Streamlined Access to Resources

Companies can greatly benefit from the integration of Viva Engage and Teams, as it enables employees to easily access important data residing in each application. This eliminates the need for staff members to switch between different platforms and makes it easier for them to collaborate and share knowledge. In addition, Teams' search capabilities can be utilized within Viva Engage to find files that are relevant to the current situation.

Companies can greatly benefit from having Microsoft Teams integrated with Viva Engage, as it enhances worker engagement, communication, and collaboration. By facilitating easy access to community activities within Teams, the integration can help employees remain productive and connected. The integration of Viva Engage and Teams can help enhance the digital workspace by providing centralized notifications, making it easier for staff members to access resources, and participating in more events. The synergy between the two applications can also help boost employee satisfaction and company success.

SharePoint Online

With Microsoft's powerful content collaboration and management platform, SharePoint Online, organizations can easily integrate Viva Engage with their existing infrastructure. This allows them to enhance their employee engagement and manage their content repositories.

The integration of Viva Engage and SharePoint Online will allow organizations to easily access and share valuable content, which will promote collaboration and knowledge sharing. Moreover, the latter's search capabilities will enable employees to find relevant content within the platform, making it easier for them to find resources that can assist them in their roles.

This section covers the features of Viva Engage **Conversations** and **Highlights**, which can be utilized to enhance the collaboration capabilities of your Microsoft 365 platform.

The web part of Viva Engage, which is called **Conversations**, as shown in Figure 4-8, features new innovations such as the ability to start a discussion with any post or poll and mark the best answers from SharePoint. By adding conversations to various internal sites, such as HR, leadership, IT, and communities, you can help your employees ask questions, share best practices, and get answers. The latest version of the Conversations web part features a few new innovations:

- The new Conversations web component features a variety of conversation types and an interactive experience.

- The new web part is designed to provide a rich media preview and visual treatment for polls, questions, and praise.

- The new Conversations publisher allows users to create and manage their own conversations.

- The new web part allows you to create multiple types of Viva Engage posts, such as questions and polls.

- Users can now upload pictures and other files to new conversations and reply to them in Microsoft SharePoint.

- You can use rich text in messages that have been created using the SharePoint platform.

- Manager actions within Viva Engage can be made using features such as Pin a Conversation, Close Conversation, and Mark Best Answer.

- The new home feed features a more relevant and personalized conversation start option.

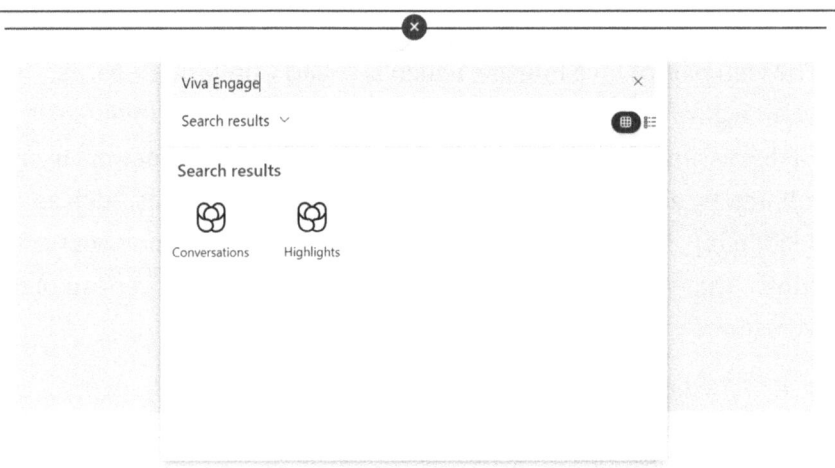

Figure 4-8. *Viva Engage Conversations web part and Highlights web part*

The new web part delivers an interactive and visually compelling experience. To accommodate this, the length of conversations will most likely increase, and the height of the part will also be adjusted. Site administrators can set the web part's height to reduce the number of conversations on a page if it gets too long.

To add a Viva Engage web part to a modern page in SharePoint, go to the Edit menu and select the option that says "Add a web part":

- To add a new web part, go to the top or bottom of the page and click the circled plus sign. You can then search for Viva Engage and choose the Conversations web part from the drop-down list.

- To view the most recent conversations in a particular group, go to the group's section and click the "Show Recent Conversations" button. On the other hand, to view the most recent conversations in a topic, go to the "Show Recent Conversations" section and click the "Show Topics" button.

- To find a source, go to the search box, then enter the group, user, or topic that you want to see.

- To determine the number of conversations that will be shown, select 4 to 8, based on the size of the web part that you want to use on your page.

Post a page and users can follow and reply to the conversations that have been created as shown in Figure 4-9.

Figure 4-9. *Conversations web part in SharePoint Online*

Use the Viva Engage **Highlights** web part for those who want to quickly overview the conversations happening in the platform.

To add a Viva Engage highlights web part to a modern page in SharePoint, go to the top right of the page and click "Edit":

- On the left side of the page, click the "Add Modern Web Part" button and then select the "Viva Engage" icon from the drop-down list. You can also search for the Viva Engage icon and add it to a page using the circled plus sign.

- If you're creating a new Viva Engage web part on a site that has a group or community associated with it, it will automatically add the group to the site's directory. If you want to search for a group, go to the "Add a Group" page and click "Search."

- The top conversations are the most talked about topics in the group. The latest conversations are those that have recently been talked about. You can also narrow the conversations by choosing only those that you want to display. To get the URL for each topic, go to Viva Engage.

- Post a new message to a group using the Post to Viva
  Engage feature. Users can then go to the group's page
  and select the post they want to see. They can also go to
  the web part's top-right corner and look for all the posts
  that are related to the group as shown in Figure 4-10.
  Unfortunately, if you add a comment below the text,
  it will not appear in the conversation as it is only on
  the page.

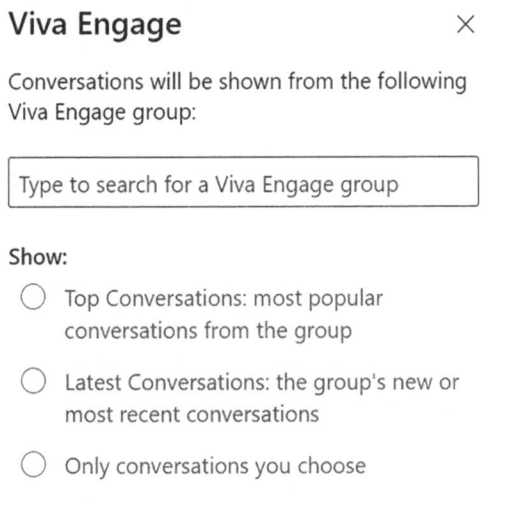

Figure 4-10. *Choose options from the Highlights web part of*
Viva Engage

The integration of Viva Engage and SharePoint Online provides employees with a variety of benefits, such as easy access to documents and videos from within the former's communities. It also promotes efficient collaboration and knowledge sharing. The ability to quickly find and retrieve relevant content using the search capabilities of Microsoft's SharePoint platform and the interactive discussions of Viva Engage enables organizations to improve their productivity and create a more collaborative digital workspace.

The integration of SharePoint Online and Viva Engage will help promote a culture of continuous improvement and learning, as workers will be able to easily contribute to and receive benefits from the shared knowledge. The integration will also help organizations reduce silos and improve their workforce productivity.

Outlook

Microsoft Outlook is a widely used email and calendar application in Microsoft 365. By integrating Viva Engage with Outlook, users can engage with their communities directly from their email inboxes. Employees can receive notifications about community activities, respond to posts, and even create new posts without leaving Outlook. This integration streamlines the engagement process, ensuring that employees remain connected to their communities while managing their daily communications. Additionally, calendar integration allows users to schedule and join community events directly from Outlook, making it easier to participate in webinars, town halls, and other engagement activities.

Work with Viva Engage using Outlook. Users of Microsoft Outlook can now easily interact with Viva Engage through polls, questions, praise, and conversations. This feature allows them to continue working on email while maintaining their social interactions and collaborating with their colleagues. Users can easily work with Viva Engage in their Outlook inbox using various platforms such as Windows, Mac, iOS, and Android.

Users can post their storyline using Outlook as shown in Figures 4-11a and 4-11b.

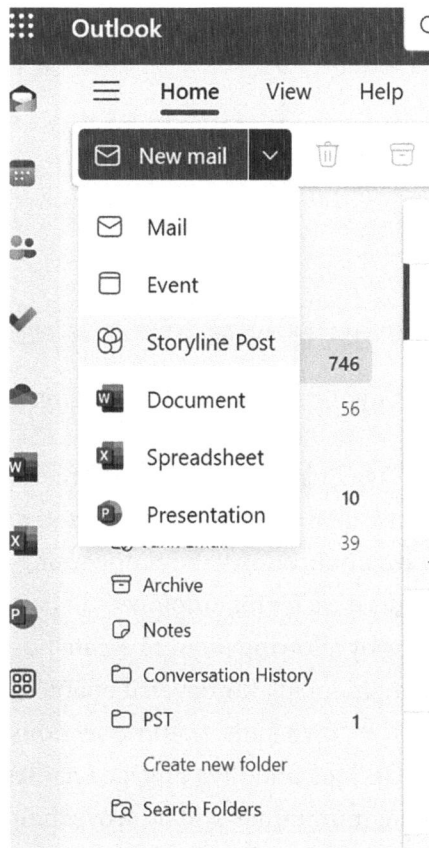

Figure 4-11a. *Storyline Post option in Outlook*

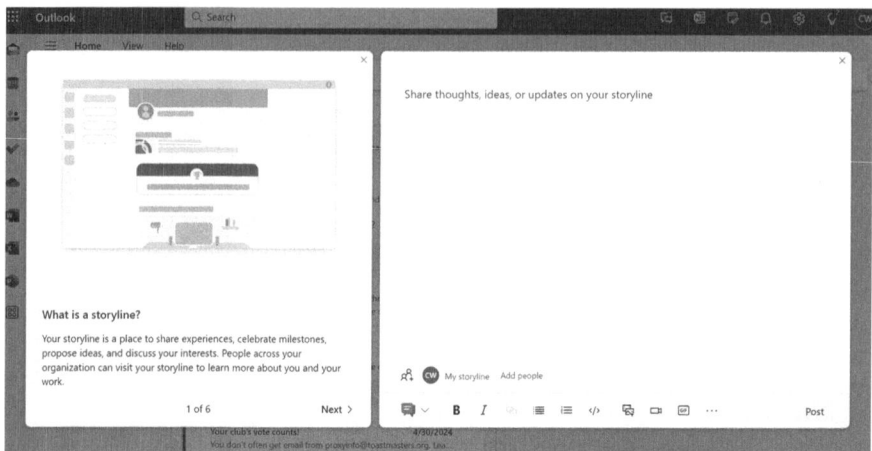

Figure 4-11b. *Publish your storyline in Viva Engage through Outlook*

The integration of Viva Engage and Outlook provides employees with a more effective and convenient way to stay connected to their communities. It allows them to receive notifications about upcoming events and updates in their inboxes. It makes it easier for employees to participate in content sharing and discussions by allowing them to create posts or respond to them without leaving their email. Moreover, it enables users to easily join community events such as town halls, training sessions, and webinars.

The integration of Outlook and Viva Engage enables employees to stay connected to their communities and improve their productivity by making it easier for them to participate in various activities. It also helps them develop better communication skills and boost their involvement in their organizations. The integration of Outlook and Viva Engage will create a more collaborative and flexible digital workspace, which will help employees feel more engaged and connected.

Power Automate

Formerly called Microsoft Flow, Power Automate is a tool that enables users to automate tasks between different apps and services, and it works seamlessly with Viva Engage. This integration allows organizations to reduce manual work and improve their productivity by eliminating redundant tasks and communicating with their employees in real time. For instance, by integrating Power Automate into project management, users can post weekly updates to the community using Viva Engage.

Using Power Automate, we can post a message to Viva Engage (Yammer), and this is illustrated as follows.

Log in to Power Automate, create a manually triggering flow, add Office 365 Outlook as a new step, and add action to send an email as shown in Figure 4-12a. Under Group ID, update the name of the Viva Engage community where you would like to publish the message as announcement as shown in Figure 4-12b.

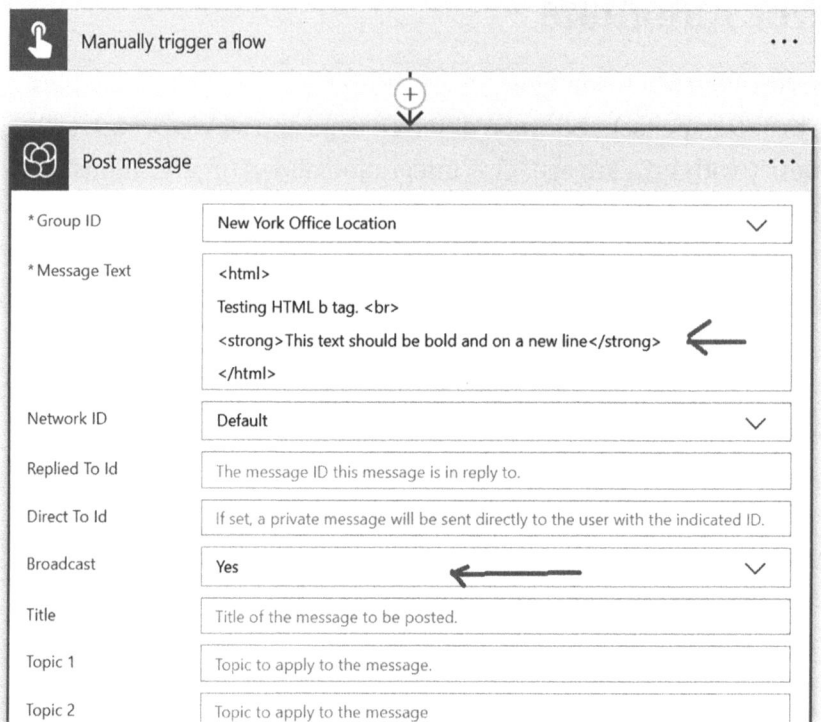

Figure 4-12a. *Power Automate to publish a message into Viva Engage*

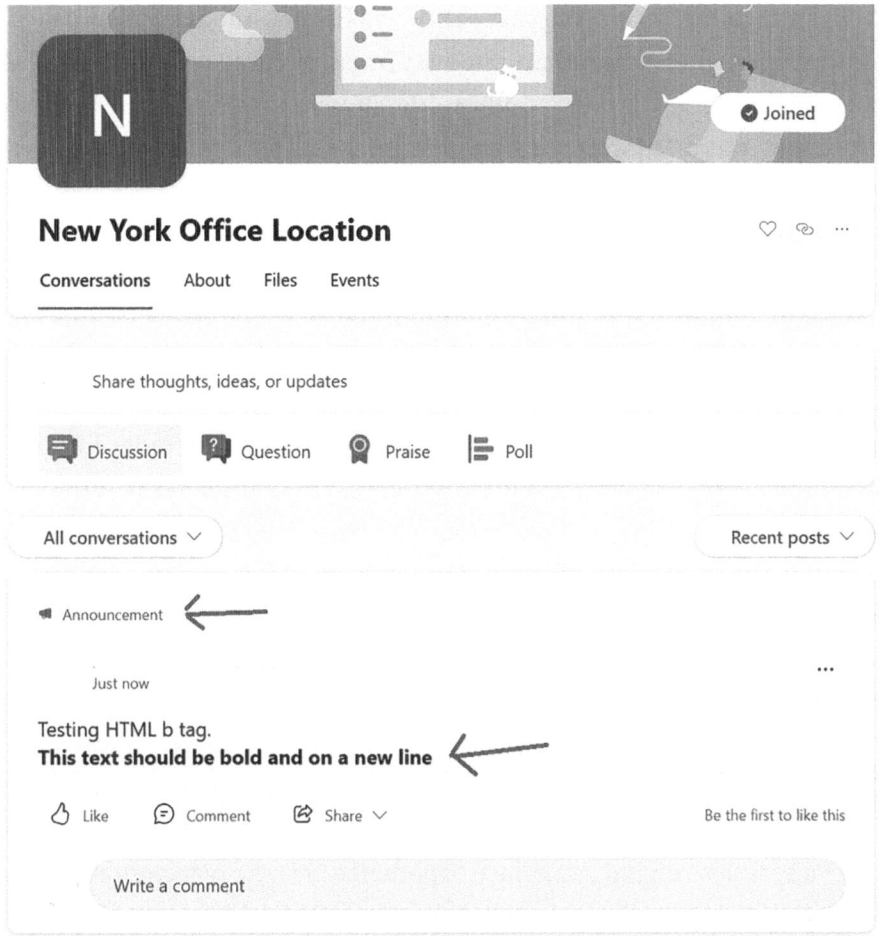

Figure 4-12b. *Announcement published in Viva Engage using Power Automate*

By integrating Power Automate and Viva Engage, organizations can improve their efficiency and productivity by automating routine tasks. This includes managing the community moderation in Viva Engage, responding to frequent queries, and posting regular updates. This eliminates the need for manual intervention and ensures that communication is constant. For instance, by integrating project updates from other applications into Viva Engage, users can be notified without the need for manual intervention. In addition, notifications about community events or activities can also be automated, allowing employees to stay engaged and on track.

Through the integration of Viva Engage and Power Automate, organizations can create a unified digital ecosystem that includes third-party applications and Microsoft 365 services. This eliminates manual intervention and helps employees focus on more creative and strategic activities. The integration of Power Automate and Viva Engage enables organizations to improve their efficiency and productivity by automating routine tasks. It can also help them create a more collaborative work environment.

With this, we have concluded the chapter where we have explored how Viva Engage integrates with other Microsoft 365 tools and services, such as Microsoft Copilot, Teams, SharePoint, Outlook, and Power Automate to create a seamless digital workplace experience across organizations, and we have experienced the benefits of each integration. In the upcoming chapter, we will explore Viva Engage in remote work environments, which include building virtual communities, remote onboarding and training, best practices for remote engagement, and measuring remote engagement.

CHAPTER 5

Remote Working Using Viva Engage

In the previous chapter, we have discovered how Viva Engage integrates with other Microsoft 365 tools and services, such as Microsoft Copilot, Teams, SharePoint, Outlook, and Power Automate, to create a seamless digital workplace experience across organizations, and we have seen benefits of each integration. In this chapter, we will explore Viva Engage for remote work environments, which includes building virtual communities, remote onboarding and training, best practices for remote engagement, and finally measuring remote engagement.

Introduction

Even though many employees have returned to work following the pandemic, the way they work is still significantly different from what it was before. Many companies have shifted to hybrid and remote work arrangements. The need to engage and connect with workers has become more critical as organizations look to improve their employee experience. Having to work from home can be very isolating for many employees. Technology can't replicate the in-person work experience, but it can help make remote work more bearable. One of the most important factors that companies can consider when it comes to implementing a remote

© The Editor(s) (if applicable) and The Author(s),
under exclusive license to APress Media, LLC, part of Springer Nature 2024
C. Waghmare, *Engage, Excel, and Elevate with Microsoft Viva Engage*, Apress Pocket Guides,
https://doi.org/10.1007/979-8-8688-0766-4_5

work solution is the integration of Microsoft Viva Engage. This solution is designed to help employees stay connected and organized.

The emergence of the new normal is starting to unfold, and it is no longer possible to predict what will happen in the future as we had experienced COVID-19. However, I think that we will look back on this period of history and see how it unfolded in the same way that we did with the 20th century "postwar" and "prewar" eras. For future generations, this is the kind of context that will allow them to talk about the technical transformation of the world. I believe emergence because it is likely that this virus will not be able to be eliminated. It is believed that it kicked off the fourth industrial revolution.

The rapid emergence and evolution of new technologies in 2020 was a major factor that affected businesses. It was also a time of change that impacted the wellness and well-being of employees. Many of them were not used to the changes brought about by the new technologies and were not able to adapt to them. The rise of home schooling and the increasing popularity of Teams calls have led to the evolution of open plan living. However, these days, architects are starting to rethink the design of home spaces to accommodate more dual-purpose rooms and quiet areas.

The year 2021 will focus on the continued evolution of the tools and methods that were used to implement remote working. These tools are designed to enable businesses to transform their operations and create a more productive and engaging environment. However, the changing nature of the working environment also poses three new challenges. Firstly, it has become a place where employees can gather, but it no longer serves as a central hub for their culture. Employees need to develop a sense of belonging and loyalty to adapt to the new environment. Managers also need to be able to help their subordinates work more efficiently to look after their well-being and productivity. In the "pre-COVID-19" era, it was easy for managers to see how stressful it was for team members, but now it is more difficult to develop insights into how to improve their performance.

In response to this, Microsoft has launched Viva Engage, a new platform that is designed to help employees create a more productive and engaged environment. It will be available in the summer months and is aimed at addressing these issues. The goal of the new platform is to help employees improve their experience and develop a better understanding of their work environment. It is also designed to help them interact with their HR and culture. It is integrated with Microsoft Teams so that it can become part of their regular work environment.

In 2020 during COVID period, most of us across the globe adopted Teams for various forms of communication, such as video, chat, and meetings. They were then able to use the underlying platform to create a more digital-centric work environment. In the latter part of the year, the company introduced Viva Engage, which was designed to provide a single solution that would allow employees to create a more hybrid experience.

How to Use Viva Engage While Working from Home

One of the key components of Microsoft Viva, which aims to improve employee engagement and knowledge, is Viva Engage. It creates a vibrant online community that enables employees to stay connected and share ideas. It works seamlessly with other offerings from Microsoft 365. We will tap on the following areas to explore Viva Engage in work from home environments:

- Setting Up Viva Engage for Remote Work

- Effective Communication Strategies

- Enhancing Collaboration

- Fostering Engagement and Inclusion

- Enhancing Productivity

101

- Supporting Well-Being and Work-Life Balance

- Building a Strong Remote Work Culture

- Measuring Success and Improvement

Setting Up Viva Engage for Remote Work

Initially, setting up the Viva Engage network involves account setup and access and profile completion in Viva Engage. Further, it involves integration with Teams, SharePoint, and Outlook.

- **Account Setup and Access**

  - **Signing Up**: To start using Viva Engage, your company's IT department must have an active subscription for it. This includes the application and the dashboard for Microsoft 365. You can access it through the application or the dashboard.

  - **Profile Completion**: Your professional profile is very important to make connections with your company's employees. It should include a photo, your job title, and a brief bio. Having this information helps them recognize and connect with you.

- **Integrating with Microsoft 365**

  - **Teams Integration:** When you integrate Viva Engage with Microsoft Teams, you'll have a seamless communication experience. It will allow you to access the communities directly from the platform and take part in discussions. You'll also be able to stay updated with the latest developments.

- **SharePoint Integration**: One of the most important factors that you should consider when it comes to implementing a new project is the integration of Microsoft's SharePoint platform with Viva Engage. This will allow you to easily share documents and work more effectively.

- **Outlook Integration**: You can also integrate Viva Engage into Outlook so that you can receive notifications about the latest activities and discussions in the community. This eliminates the need for you to check the platform frequently.

Effective Communication Strategies

Communication is very important for successful remote work. With the help of Viva Engage, remote teams can easily communicate with one another. This involves creating and managing communities and posting and interacting.

Creating and Managing Communities

- **Community Creation**: Creating distinct communities for different groups or interests enables information sharing and discussions. These communities serve as dedicated areas that focus on specific topics, facilitating easy access to relevant content and facilitating engagement with the appropriate individuals.

- **Moderation and Guidelines**: To ensure that the discussions are conducted in a civil and productive manner, community managers should be assigned to oversee them. They should also enforce guidelines to minimize conflicts and encourage positive interactions.

- **Announcements**: The announcement feature can help disseminate important updates. It can be used to place announcements at the top of the feed for quick visibility.

Posting and Interacting

- **Regular Updates**: Regularly posting announcements about projects, business news, and other important topics keeps everyone in the loop. This form of communication promotes trust and transparency among remote teams.

- **Comments and Reactions**: Interact with your team members and encourage them to comment on or react to posts, which can foster a more engaged environment and make them feel valued and heard. Feedback and comments can help you assess the effectiveness of your messages.

- **Polls and Surveys**: Surveys and polls can be used to gather opinions and make decisions. They can be used to ask for feedback on different topics, such as employee satisfaction and new initiatives. This type of participatory approach can foster a sense of involvement and ownership among the team.

Enhancing Collaboration

Effective collaboration is crucial for remote teams to work together efficiently. With the integration of Viva Engage with Microsoft 365, remote teams can work more effectively. This involves document sharing and collaboration and project management and task coordination.

Document Sharing and Collaboration

- **SharePoint Integration**: Through the integration of Microsoft 365 with Viva Engage, remote teams can easily share documents from their SharePoint libraries. This allows them to promote collaboration and knowledge sharing.

- **Co-authoring**: One of the most important factors that businesses consider when it comes to implementing effective collaboration is the ability to real-time co-authoring. This feature allows team members to work on a single document at the same time, which is ideal for projects.

- **Version Control**: One of the most important steps that businesses should take when implementing effective collaboration is to maintain version control. This ensures that all team members are working with the latest information. Doing so can help boost overall productivity and avoid errors.

Project Management and Task Coordination

- **Planner Integration**: With the integration of Microsoft Planner with Viva Engage, remote teams can now easily assign tasks, track their progress, and manage their projects' timelines. This feature can help keep them organized and on track, ensuring effective collaboration.

- **Task Updates**: To ensure that the team is still aligned and informed, regularly post updates about the status of projects and tasks. Transparency in the progress of tasks fosters accountability and lets everyone know of their responsibilities.

- **Feedback Loops**: Gather feedback from the community through discussions about the project's deliverables. This feedback loop can help ensure that the final product meets the expectations of the team.

Fostering Engagement and Inclusion

When it comes to maintaining a positive work environment, it's important to keep the employees engaged and included. With the help of Viva Engage, remote teams can create a more inclusive environment. This involves virtual events and activities and encouraging participation.

Virtual Events and Activities

- **Webinars and Training**: Through training sessions and webinars, Viva Engage can help its remote employees develop their skills and keep them motivated. These events also provide them with an opportunity to share their knowledge.

- **Social Events**: Virtual events can be organized such as coffee chats, team building activities, and game sessions. These types of events can help strengthen the bonds among the team members and provide them with a much-needed break.

- **Recognition Programs**: To celebrate the achievements of its employees, Viva Engage can host recognition events. These programs can help boost the morale of the team members and show appreciation for their hard work.

Encouraging Participation

- **Inclusive Discussions**: Viva Engage can foster a more inclusive atmosphere by encouraging every member of the team to share their ideas and thoughts. A diverse perspective can help produce novel approaches and enhance the work atmosphere.

- **Feedback Mechanisms**: To improve the experience of the remote team members, Viva Engage can implement feedback mechanisms such as surveys and suggestion boxes. By actively seeking out feedback, you're able to show that you value the opinions of the team members.

- **Diverse Content**: The company's content should appeal to varying interests and promote respect and inclusivity. Highlighting certain topics, like professional development and company values, will make sure that everybody finds it engaging and relevant.

Enhancing Productivity

With Viva Engage, remote teams can focus on and stay productive. It includes various features to help them work more efficiently. This involves time management and scheduling and task automation.

Time Management and Scheduling

- **Calendar Integration**: With the integration of Viva Engage with Team Calendars and Outlook, remote teams can easily plan and manage their meetings and other important activities.

- **Reminders and Notifications**: You can set up notifications and reminders for important events and tasks. These help keep the team focused and on track and prevent them from missing out on deadlines.

- **Prioritization**: Through community discussions, remote teams can easily prioritize their projects and tasks. This helps them focus on the most critical ones and achieve their goals more effectively.

Task Automation

- **Power Automate Integration**: You can integrate Viva Engage into Power Automate, which will allow you to automate various routine tasks, like posting updates, moderating the community, and responding to queries. This eliminates manual work and helps maintain consistent communication.

- **Workflow Optimization**: By integrating Viva Engage with third-party applications and Microsoft 365 services, workflows can be streamlined, resulting in increased efficiency and decreased time spent on repetitive activities.

- **Continuous Improvement**: To ensure that your automated processes remain relevant and effective, regularly review them. This can help you maintain high levels of productivity and adapt to changes in requirements.

Supporting Well-Being and Work-Life Balance

Working remotely can blur the lines between personal and professional life. It's important to support employees' well-being and promote a work-life balance. This involves mental health and wellness and flexibility and autonomy.

Mental Health and Wellness

- **Wellness Programs**: Through Viva Engage, you can promote various programs that help employees improve their well-being, such as mental health resources and meditation sessions.

- **Stress Management**: Share coping resources and encourage discussions about stress management techniques. Open lines about mental health can foster a more caring and supportive atmosphere.

- **Breaks and Downtime:** Promote the importance of taking regular breaks and downtime to prevent burnout. Encourage employees to step away from their screens and engage in relaxing activities.

Flexibility and Autonomy

- **Flexible Schedules**: Employees should be supported with flexible work arrangements, as it allows them to focus on their personal responsibilities while also working. This can improve their job satisfaction and enable them to effectively manage their time.

- **Autonomy**: Allowing employees to manage their schedules and tasks can foster a sense of accountability and ownership.

- **Work-Life Integration**: To encourage integration at work, accommodate personal commitments. Acknowledgment of personal significance enhances a more conducive atmosphere for a more balanced work setting.

Building a Strong Remote Work Culture

A strong work culture is vital for success. With Viva Engage, you can build and sustain this through regular communication and support. This involves core values and vision and continuous learning and development.

Core Values and Vision

- **Communicating Core Values**: Through Viva Engage, an organization's core values and vision can be communicated regularly. It helps employees align themselves with the company's mission.

- **Leading by Example**: By participating in Viva Engage communities, leaders can show their commitment to the organization's values and goals. They can influence the culture of the company.

- **Recognizing Contributions**: Acknowledge and celebrate the contributions of staff members to the success of the organization. Doing so helps strengthen the company's sense of community and reinforces individual significance.

Continuous Learning and Development

- **Learning Opportunities**: Support staff members' professional development by hosting training sessions, webinars, and events. Doing so helps keep them motivated and engaged.

- **Mentorship Programs**: Professional development and knowledge transfer can be facilitated through mentorship initiatives. It also helps strengthen team bonds and promotes personal growth.

- **Innovation and Creativity:** The company can encourage creativity and innovation by providing a platform where staff members can share their ideas. A culture of innovation fosters adaptableness and constant improvement.

Measuring Success and Improvement

To maximize remote work effectiveness, it's crucial to regularly assess the strategy and strive for continual improvement. This involves key performance indicators (KPIs) and continuous improvement.

Key Performance Indicators (KPIs)

- **Defining KPIs:** KPIs can be established to measure the effectiveness of remote work programs. These can include project outcomes, employee satisfaction, productivity, and engagement levels.

- **Regular Reviews:** To ensure continuous improvement, review the KPIs regularly. This can help address issues immediately.

- **Feedback and Adjustments:** Make changes to remote work programs after collecting feedback from staff members. Feedback can help keep the strategies relevant.

Continuous Improvement

- **Iterative Process:** Adopt a process-based approach to remote work, wherein strategies are continuously refined and improved through the feedback and evaluation of performance. This promotes resilience and adaptability.

- **Best Practices**: To motivate and inspire staff members, an organization should share success stories and best practices. Highlighting successful initiatives can encourage experimentation and adoption.

- **Learning from Challenges**: To create remote work solutions that are more robust and efficient, learn from setbacks and difficulties. Embracing growth mindsets can help turn difficult situations into opportunities to improve.

There are many opportunities and challenges that come with working from home. With Microsoft Viva Engage, you can take advantage of these by creating a productive and engaging work environment. It helps organizations establish and maintain a strong work culture, promote inclusion and engagement, and enhance communication. To ensure that remote work remains viable and advantageous in the future, one must continuously improve and adapt.

Best Practices for Working from Home

As more people choose to work from home, it is important that they follow best practices to improve their productivity and maintain a work-life balance. This section provides a variety of strategies that can help them succeed using Viva Engage. Let's understand best practices using the following points:

- Setting Up Your Workspace

- Establishing a Routine

- Enhancing Productivity

- Maintaining Communication and Collaboration

- Fostering Engagement and Team Cohesion

- Continuous Improvement

Setting Up Your Workspace

This includes designating a dedicated workspace and adopting technology and tools.

Designating a Dedicated Workspace

- Create a boundary between your personal life and work by choosing a specific area in your home. This will help you keep yourself mentally focused on work while you're in it.

- Make sure that your workspace is designed to accommodate your needs. It should feature a comfortable chair, desk height, and sufficient lighting to improve focus and reduce strain. Having an ideal workspace can help boost your productivity and improve your physical well-being.

- A quiet area is ideal for minimizing distractions. You can also try using headphones or playing music to keep yourself focused.

Adopting Technology and Tools

- When working remotely, having a fast Internet connection is important to ensure uninterrupted work.

- You must have all the essential equipment for your job, such as a computer, a headset, a webcam, and other specialized tools. Regularly maintaining and updating these items will ensure that you do not encounter technical issues.

- You should also use collaboration tools such as Microsoft Teams and Slack to keep in touch with your team. Be knowledgeable about these to maximize their capabilities.

Establishing a Routine

This includes consistent schedule and balancing work and personal life.

Consistent Schedule

- Follow regular work hours to create a psychological structure and a normalized environment. Ensure that your team is informed about your schedule and availability.

- Establish a routine that will allow you to wake up and start your day with a positive start. This can include a nutritious breakfast, reading, or exercising. It will help you shift into a more productive state of mind.

- Break time should be scheduled every day to allow you to recharge and take breaks. One method you can use is the Pomodoro technique, which requires working for 25 minutes before taking a break of about 5 minutes. For lunch, take a longer break to get away from the computer.

Balancing Work and Personal Life

- Make sure that you clearly state the boundaries between your personal life and work. You should avoid working in areas that are conducive to relaxation, such as a bedroom or living room.

- You should create an end-of-day routine, which will allow you to say goodbye to your work for the day. It can include simple activities like going for a walk, closing the computer, or tidying up your workspace. This will help you unwind and mentally transition from your work to your personal life.

- You should also communicate with household members about your schedule and requirements. Having a set of ground rules will help minimize interruptions at work.

Enhancing Productivity

This includes time management and minimizing distractions.

Time Management

- You can organize and prioritize your tasks using a task management system. Some of the tools that can help you do this include Asana, Trello, and Microsoft To Do.

- Use focus techniques to categorize your tasks into priority groups. Doing so will help you prioritize and manage your time efficiently.

- Batch processing involves grouping related tasks and completing them in batches. This strategy can help minimize the mental strain of switching tasks between different categories and improve your efficiency.

Minimizing Distractions

- To limit your digital distractions, turn off notifications that aren't essential and use apps that block websites. Also, set specific times to check your messages and emails.

- Physical distractions can keep you from being able to focus on your work. Having a clutter-free and organized workspace helps you work more efficiently.

- Setting specific times throughout the day can help you focus on important work while avoiding interruptions. It can also help you communicate with your team about expectations.

Maintaining Communication and Collaboration

This includes regular check-ins, effective use of collaboration tools, and clear communication.

Regular Check-Ins

- Microsoft Teams are ideal for facilitating communication and working collaboratively. They can be used to create channels for groups and projects to share ideas and files.

- Work collaboratively using tools like OneDrive and SharePoint. These allow teams to work on a single document at the same time and keep track of changes.

- You can also integrate other task management tools such as Asana and Planner into your Microsoft Teams platform. These tools can help you keep track of the progress of your project and assign tasks.

Effective Use of Collaboration

- With Microsoft Teams, you can work seamlessly with your team and allow groups and projects to share files and discuss topics.

- You can also use tools such as OneDrive and SharePoint to collaborate on documents in real time. This feature allows multiple people to work on a specific document at the exact same time.

- You can integrate other task management applications like Asana or Planner into your work platform, allowing you to keep track of projects and tasks.

Tools and Clear Communication

- To avoid misunderstandings, write clear and concise messages in a way that makes them easier to read. This can be achieved by bullet points, headings, and other formatting.

- When in meetings or discussions, try to practice active listening, which involves paying attention to what's being said and asking clarifying questions.

- Acknowledge and reward your teammates. Give your team members regular recognition and feedback, as well as constructive criticism, to help them grow.

Fostering Engagement and Team Cohesion

This includes virtual team building, encouraging participation, and supporting well-being.

Virtual Team Building

- Virtual social activities can be organized for team members to connect and maintain a sense of community. These include online games and coffee chats.

- Bringing together teams for competitions or team challenges can help foster a more collaborative environment. These may include creative projects, fitness tests, or trivia quizzes.

- Team members can celebrate individual achievements and milestones through shout-outs or virtual events. Acknowledgment of such accomplishments can boost one's motivation and morale.

Encouraging Participation

- Create an inclusive environment by encouraging members to participate in group discussions and talk about their ideas. Everyone should feel valued and heard.

- Open communication channels allow members to share their thoughts and provide feedback. To facilitate such conversations, one can use tools such as Slack or Teams.

- Employee surveys are also useful to gather feedback about the work experience of remote employees. These insights can be used to address any issues and improve the company's operations.

Supporting Well-Being

- Providing access to mental health support and resources can help team members feel valued and supported. Information about programs and activities that can help one manage their stress can be shared.

- Regularly taking breaks can help prevent burnout. Encourage staff members to take breaks and engage in nonwork-related leisure pursuits.

- To help employees achieve work-life balance, the company should provide flexible work arrangements. It should also encourage staff members to set boundaries and prioritize their well-being.

Continuous Improvement

This includes gathering feedback, adapting and evolving, and training and development.

Gathering Feedback

- Surveys are frequently conducted to gather feedback about remote work methods, tools, and the overall experience of employees. Feedback may help identify areas of improvement and enable adjustments.

- Town hall meetings or forums can be established to allow employees to share their suggestions and thoughts. Such forums and discussions can foster honest communication and encourage continuous improvement.

- A suggestion box may be created to allow employees to share their ideas about how to improve remote work. These suggestions should then be evaluated and may be used to enhance the workplace.

Adapting and Evolving

- Follow the latest best practices and trends in remote work by joining professional networks, attending webinars, and reading articles.

- Be adaptable and open to change. You should also be able to modify your remote work methods to accommodate changes in requirements.

- Follow the recommendations of your peers and evaluate your own experience with remote work. You can then improve the efficiency and effectiveness of your work by identifying areas of weakness and implementing fixes.

Training and Development

- Providing continuous learning opportunities can help employees develop their skills and knowledge. They can access online courses, conferences, and training initiatives that can help them improve their abilities.

- Support career advancement and growth by establishing mentorship initiatives. By pairing experienced workers with fresh recruits, the two parties can provide each other with valuable insight and encouragement.

- Encouraging knowledge sharing through various means, such as virtual workshops, internal forums, and lunch-and-learn programs, can help foster a culture of collaboration and learning.

Leveraging Technology

This includes advanced collaboration tools and automation and efficiency.

Advanced Collaboration Tools

- Enhance collaboration and streamline project management through the use of software such as Microsoft Project or Asana.

- Use video conferencing software such as Google Meet, Microsoft Teams, and Zoom to improve collaboration and keep in touch with colleagues.

- Cloud storage providers such as Dropbox, Google Drive, and OneDrive can help ensure the accessibility and secure storage of files.

Automation and Efficiency

- Use automation tools such as Microsoft Power Automate to automatically perform repetitive tasks. They can help reduce the amount of time spent on manual work.

- Use tools that help boost efficiency, like time tracking apps, appointment schedulers, and productivity boosters, such as Focus@Will.

- Using data analytics tools can help organizations monitor and analyze their productivity. They can then make informed decisions and improve their workflows.

All the best practices are possible using Viva Engage. There are many unique opportunities and challenges when it comes to working from home. Viva Engage ensures that you have a productive and balanced work experience by following these best practices. These can help you establish a conducive environment and keep improving. Having a dedicated workspace and maintaining a consistent schedule can help you keep up with the work. Prioritize your well-being and leverage technology to do your homework more sustainably.

Building Virtual Communities Using Viva Engage

Virtual communities are essential for fostering collaboration and connection within the workplace, especially in hybrid or remote environments. With the help of Microsoft Viva Engage, you can easily create and manage these types of communities. This guide will teach you how to effectively utilize this feature. The following are the steps to build virtual communities using Viva Engage:

- **Define the Purpose and Goals**: Your virtual community's primary goal should be identified. Do you want to foster innovation, encourage employee morale, or improve knowledge sharing? Your target audience should be identified, and this should include the various departments and teams within the organization.

- **Set Up the Community**: Viva Engage can help you create a new community. Its name should reflect its purpose and connect with your intended audience. You can customize the settings to meet your requirements. You can decide whether it will be private or public, and you can set the permissions to manage the content and notifications.

- **Design an Engaging Structure**: The community should be organized around clear topics and categories to facilitate discussions and facilitate the discovery of relevant content. You can use pinned posts to highlight important announcements or other key information.

- **Promote Active Participation**: New members should be welcomed with a pinned post that explains the community's mission and guidelines. Post regularly updated questions and articles to encourage participation and keep the community engaged. You can also highlight interesting topics by sharing them with the community.

- **Share Your Resources, Knowledge, and Experience**: Urge members to connect with one another and share their personal experiences, resources, or knowledge.

- **Acknowledge and Reward Those Who Share**: Fostering a Culture of Sharing.

- **Facilitate Meaningful Interactions**: Moderators can be assigned to moderate discussions to ensure that they are respectful and productive. They can also ensure that the community is following guidelines. Inclusiveness: Ensure that everyone in the community feels valued and accepted. Reinforce diversity by creating a safe environment that enables everyone to speak their minds without judgment. Acknowledge and thank members for their postings. Interact with them by offering feedback, expressing your appreciation, and celebrating their contributions.

- **Leverage Integration with Microsoft 365**: Microsoft Teams and Viva Engage can be integrated to allow users to access the latter's community discussions in the former's channels. This will help organizations integrate community interactions into their daily workflows. You can utilize OneDrive and SharePoint to collaborate and share documents. You can also link relevant files and resources in community posts. You can use Outlook to send notifications to members about community events and updates.

- **Use Multimedia and Interactive Content**: Enhance community posts with rich media content, such as images and videos, to make them more engaging. You can also create interactive elements by conducting surveys, live events, and polls to gather feedback and stimulate discussion.

- **Monitor and Evaluate Community Health**: Follow the community's analytics to get a deeper understanding of its activities and content. This will allow you to adjust and improve the experience. A feedback loop is established to allow members to share their thoughts about the community's operations. You can regularly seek members' feedback through direct messages or surveys and then act on their suggestions.

- **Foster a Sense of Belonging**: To foster an inclusive and positive community culture, you should promote core values like openness, collaboration, and respect. To build community unity and pride, recognize and celebrate achievements such as reaching a particular number of individuals or attaining significant goals.

- **Encourage Cross-Community Collaboration**: Promote cross-community projects within the organization. Incent members to get involved in such initiatives to foster a more connected community. You can also organize training sessions and workshops that involve several communities. These experiences can help break down silos and foster knowledge sharing.

When it comes to creating a virtual community, it takes a lot of planning and dedication to ensure that it is successful. This can be achieved through the establishment of clear goals and an environment that is conducive to collaboration. In addition to being able to create engaging and supportive communities, Viva Engage can also help organizations improve their remote workforce productivity and satisfaction.

Remote Onboarding and Training with Viva Engage

The onboarding and training process for Microsoft Viva Engage is designed to help employees connect with their organization's culture and goals. It starts with introducing new staff members to the platform, which provides a digital space for discussions and learning.

New hires are introduced to the platform through various features, such as polls and Q&A sessions. They are also encouraged to actively participate in the company's culture and are introduced to the idea of knowledge sharing, which allows them to contribute their experiences and insights to the organization's collective knowledge.

Through Viva Engage, users can build their networks and personal brand by sharing stories using their favorite social tools. It also helps them connect with their company's leaders and develop their professional identity. One of the most beneficial aspects of the platform is that it allows new employees to establish their presence immediately.

The goal of the platform is to simplify the onboarding process by consolidating all of the necessary tools and resources in one place. It also enables the creation of customized learning modules that are designed to help new hires become acquainted with the team and organizational needs. The integration of Microsoft Teams with Viva Engage allows employees to seamlessly utilize the platform.

An ongoing training process with Viva Engage can be carried out beyond the onboarding phase. The company promotes skill development and learning by providing users with numerous learning opportunities and resources. It also lets users form communities interact with coworkers through virtual events and town halls and stay updated with announcements sent to them by their devices.

The training and onboarding process with Microsoft Viva Engage can significantly simplify the HR functions of an organization. It can also help develop a more vibrant and connected workplace environment by encouraging employees to contribute to the company's collective intelligence.

The ease of use and accessibility of the Viva Engage platform make it an ideal choice for new employees. Its customizable features also help organizations customize the system to meet their specific requirements. Through the data collected by the platform, organizations can improve their training and onboarding processes.

Measuring Remote Engagement Using Viva Engage

When it comes to measuring the effectiveness of Microsoft Viva Engage's remote workforce management platform, the company's analytics capabilities can help identify how employees are engaging with the digital workspace. The first step in this process is to understand the various features of the platform.

There are various tools and resources that can help employees communicate with their remote teams and promote well-being and mental health. These examples include the Home Office Heroes community, global communication hubs, and wellness sanctuaries.

Through the various features of Viva Engage, employees can participate in team bonding, knowledge sharing, cultural exchange, and event planning. These features not only provide a sense of belonging and community, but they also aid in measuring how engaged they are.

Through the various reporting tools that are available on the platform, organizations can easily monitor the usage and adoption trends of Microsoft 365. These tools can help them identify key metrics such as the number of active users and the community engagement levels.

New features in Viva Engage allow senior executives to connect with their subordinates across different organizations. The various features of Viva Engage allow employees to connect with their leaders and other members of the company. They can also participate in Q&As and other direct connections through the platform's Leadership Corner. Other features such as storylines, announcements, and social campaigns can help employees connect with their coworkers and promote shared initiatives.

Measuring the effectiveness of Microsoft Viva Engage's remote workforce management platform involves a comprehensive analysis that combines the company's analytics capabilities with the various features of the platform. This approach can help organizations identify how their staff members are engaged and develop strategies to improve their remote workforce.

With this, we have come to the end of this chapter where we explored on how to use Viva Engage while working from home, best practices for work from home, building virtual communities, how to use Viva Engage for remote onboarding and training, and finally measuring remote engagement.

In the last chapter, we will look at ensuring accessibility and inclusivity and security and compliance considerations for Viva Engage. This chapter will cover exploring the importance of accessibility in digital platforms like Viva Engage and its impact on diverse user groups; highlighting built-in accessibility features within Viva Engage and how they can be leveraged to improve user experience for all; discussing various compliance regulations and standards that may apply to organizations using Viva Engage, such as GDPR, HIPAA, and SOC 2; and exploring the security features and controls available within Viva Engage, including data encryption, access controls, and identity management. So, stay tuned for the last chapter.

CHAPTER 6

Ensuring Accessibility and Inclusivity and Security and Compliance Considerations for Viva Engage

In the previous chapter, we talked about how to use Viva Engage to work from home. It covered various aspects of the platform, such as how it can be used to create virtual communities, manage remote training and onboarding, and measure remote engagement. In this final chapter of the book, we will cover the importance of accessibility and inclusivity in digital platforms like Viva Engage and their impact on diverse user groups; highlight built-in accessibility features within Viva Engage and how they can be leveraged to improve user experience for all; discuss various compliance regulations and standards that may apply to organizations

© The Editor(s) (if applicable) and The Author(s), 131
under exclusive license to APress Media, LLC, part of Springer Nature 2024
C. Waghmare, *Engage, Excel, and Elevate with Microsoft Viva Engage*, Apress Pocket Guides,
https://doi.org/10.1007/979-8-8688-0766-4_6

using Viva Engage, such as GDPR, HIPAA, and SOC 2; and explore the
security features and controls available within Viva Engage, including data
encryption, access controls, and identity management. Also, a personal
view and recommendations will be covered on the future of the Viva
Engage platform.

Introduction

Inclusivity and accessibility are crucial factors when creating products and
environments that are welcoming and usable for everyone. The concept
of accessibility refers to the creation of environments or products that
are designed to provide people with disabilities equal access to essential
services and information. This includes the use of Braille signs, wheelchair
ramps, and websites that are designed to be accessed by typing with a
keyboard. It ensures that individuals with disabilities have the necessary
tools and resources to engage fully. Barriers can be removed with
accessibility, allowing disabled people to engage fully.

On the other hand, inclusivity is a broader concept that entails creating
environments that are welcoming and diverse. This concept also includes
making accommodations for individuals with disabilities. In addition to
this, inclusivity encompasses considerations such as age, gender, culture,
socioeconomic status, and other factors. To foster a culture of acceptance,
inclusivity involves establishing a welcoming environment where people
feel accepted and supported. This can be achieved through various forms
of social interaction, education, and workplace policies. Inclusivity can
also be reflected in community programs and educational materials,
which ensure that everyone has an opportunity to participate.

The goal of inclusivity and accessibility is to create a society where
people of all genders, ages, and abilities can fully participate and thrive.
These principles play a vital role in various fields, such as education,
technology, and employment. To achieve this, ongoing efforts are needed
to eliminate barriers and promote equity.

Importance of Accessibility and Inclusivity in Viva Engage

Designing software with inclusivity and accessibility in mind, such as in Viva Engage, can offer numerous benefits. These can extend beyond meeting legal requirements and fostering an equitable and more engaging experience for users. The following are some key advantages of implementing accessibility and inclusivity in software such as Viva Engage:

> **Enhanced User Experience**: By making software more accessible, developers can ensure that people with disabilities can use it. This can help widen the software's appeal to a wide range of users, including those with cognitive, sensory, and motor impairments. Some of the most effective ways to improve the usability of software are its navigation features and keyboard shortcuts. These features can help people with different disabilities get the most out of it. For instance, captioned videos can help people with hearing impairments use software in noisy environments.

> **Legal and Ethical Benefits**: To avoid costly penalties and legal issues, software should follow accessibility standards set by the Web Content Accessibility Guidelines (WCAG), the Americans with Disabilities Act (ADA), or the European Accessibility Act. Emphasizing inclusivity and accessibility reinforces a company's commitment to social responsibility and ethical practices, which can enhance its reputation.

Competitive Advantage: When it comes to the market, having accessibility can set a product apart from its competitors. According to studies, loyal customers are more likely to stay with a brand if they feel valued and accommodated. Having a positive experience with software that is made more accessible can help boost customer retention and satisfaction.

Innovation and Quality: Developing accessibility-related innovations sparks new ideas that can enhance the software's overall quality. For instance, text-to-speech and voice recognition systems are being used to address various applications. Getting accessibility built into the software from the beginning can reduce the time and money spent on retrofitting later. Doing so helps maintain a high level of quality throughout the life of the software.

Social and Economic Inclusion: People with disabilities could fully participate in the workforce using accessible software. This promotes inclusion and diversity in the workplace. The design of the software should be inclusive to ensure that all team members can use it effectively. This can lead to increased collaboration and productivity. In addition to being beneficial for those with disabilities, inclusive software design also benefits everyone. It can enhance the experience of users, encourage innovation, and promote responsible and ethical practices. Doing so can result in better software and society.

A social networking platform like Viva Engage has been designed
with accessibility features that allow people with disabilities, such as
those with limited dexterity or vision, to easily use it. We want to make
sure that all your employees and leaders can benefit from its features.
With the accessibility features and settings enabled in Microsoft 365 apps,
people with disabilities can easily use the site and its various features. For
instance, they can change the colors on the screen to make it easier to
see and control the device. The settings can be customized depending on
the kind of device you have, such as Android, iOS, Windows, or Mac. The
following are some of the accessibility features enabled in Microsoft 365
apps such as Viva Engage:

- Windows 11 offers a variety of settings and features
  designed to help people with disabilities use the device.
  The Accessibility menu can be found under Settings.
  There, you can launch Narrator or Magnifier.

- Windows 11's Narrator is a built-in app that provides a
  screen reading experience. You can learn more about it
  by going to the Complete guide.

- A contrast theme can help enhance the colors on your
  screen so that you can easily see text and items. The
  Accessibility menu will show contrast themes. You can
  refer to the accessibility settings in Microsoft 365 and
  change the color contrast on Windows to get the most
  out of it.

- The Magnifier tool can magnify various parts of your
  screen content. You can set it to work for both a full and
  a lens pane.

- Without changing the resolution of your screen, you
  can adjust the text size on it.

- Changing the color and size of your mouse's pointer
  can make it easier to use. If you're new to speech
  recognition, you must set it up.

The preceding features help any user group to access the Viva
Engage platform in an easy way and create a best experience among user
communities.

Now let's look at the inclusivity aspect in Viva Engage. The Viva
Engage platform must foster an inclusive culture within the workplace
to cultivate a productive and supportive atmosphere. As companies
recognize the significance of inclusion and diversity, they must integrate
these principles into their messaging tools. Using Viva Engage, companies
can create an environment that is inclusive of all employees. This can help
boost employee engagement and innovation, as well as improve business
success. In this section, we'll talk about the many benefits of inclusive
culture that it can provide.

Creating an Inclusive Organizational Culture: The goal of Viva
Engage is to create a culture that values and respects all employees,
regardless of their abilities, backgrounds, or identity. This platform can act
as a gathering place for diverse voices, encouraging employees to share
their ideas and experiences. Ensuring that Viva Engage is welcoming
and accessible will help promote a more inclusive culture within the
workplace. In addition, it can help break down silos by encouraging open
dialogue and helping to bridge the gap between various levels of the
organization.

Enhancing Employee Engagement and Retention: An inclusive work environment can result in a higher level of commitment and engagement from employees, as it allows them to feel valued for their unique perspectives. Viva Engage can play a crucial role in this by helping workers connect with one another and with their superiors through its platform. Various features, such as social interactions, polls, and discussion forums, can be utilized to gather feedback from the company's diverse workforce. This type of engagement can boost employee morale and retention rates, as it allows workers to feel valued and supported by their employer.

Promoting Innovation Through Diverse Perspectives: The fostering of inclusive thoughts leads to innovative ideas. Viva Engage enables individuals from varying backgrounds to come together and share their perspectives, ultimately fueling fresh thinking and challenging conventional wisdom. Through an inclusive work environment, employees from different backgrounds can participate in decision-making processes and brainstorming sessions, allowing them to provide a wider range of input. Organizations can take advantage of this collective intelligence to adapt to changes in the market and remain ahead of the curve.

Building a More Equitable Workplace: By providing all employees with equal opportunities to contribute and participate, Viva Engage can help build a more equitable workplace. To ensure that it is accessible to individuals with disabilities, the platform should offer accessibility features such as keyboard navigation and a screen reader compatibility. Viva Engage should enable workers to freely convey their personal experiences and identities without the risk of discrimination or prejudice. By implementing policies and practices that are inclusive, companies can foster a more just and fairer workplace.

Facilitating Effective Communication: Inclusivity in Viva Engage can amplify the effectiveness of communication by enabling every employee to have their voice heard. This involves actively listening and responding to their suggestions. This can be achieved by implementing various features, such as dedicated areas for underrepresented groups and anonymous feedback channels. When staff members believe their suggestions and concerns are being seriously considered, their trust in the company grows, leading to more transparent and effective communication.

Supporting Diverse Employee Resource Groups (ERGs): An employee resource group (ERG) is a vital part of any organization's efforts to promote inclusion and diversity. Viva Engage can help these groups by providing them with a dedicated area for their gatherings, activities, and events. These groups can also utilize the platform to connect with their members and share resources. The support and visibility provided to ERGs can help strengthen their impact and ensure that their ideas are included in the company's wider dialogue. By facilitating their work, Viva Engage can help promote a more inclusive culture within the organization.

Enhancing Leadership Engagement: Inclusivity in Viva Engage goes beyond merely ensuring that leadership is sensitive to the diverse workforce's needs. Through the platform, leaders can reach out to their staff members directly and share updates, as well as receive feedback. This form of communication fosters accountability and connection, making it clear that leaders are dedicated to making the workplace more inclusive. Viva Engage's regular interactions between Teams and leaders can help build transparency and trust, which implies that inclusivity is a top priority for the company.

Fostering Continuous Learning and Development: An inclusive work platform like Viva Engage can help employees develop their skills and knowledge by offering various training opportunities and resources. These include leadership development courses, diversity and inclusion training, and skill-building exercises. By making these opportunities accessible through an inclusive platform, companies can ensure that all workers have the chance to advance their careers. Not only will it help individual employees, but continuous learning can also boost an organization's competitiveness and capabilities.

Measuring and Tracking Inclusivity Efforts: Viva Engage's inclusive work platform can be tracked and measured through various analytics and metrics. These tools can be used to monitor various aspects of the program, such as the participation rates, levels of engagement, and feedback from the diverse workforce. This data can be used to identify areas of improvement and highlight areas of concern. Organizations can take advantage of this data to make informed decisions and improve their efforts in fostering an inclusive culture.

Strengthening Employer Branding: An inclusive workplace is attractive to both employees and employers. By using Viva Engage to promote inclusivity, companies can improve their branding and attract high-performing individuals from diverse backgrounds. People are becoming more discerning when it comes to choosing a workplace that values diversity. Highlighting Viva Engage's inclusivity efforts, such as testimonials from employees, can elevate an organization's reputation.

Creating a Positive Social Impact: Viva Engage goes beyond the workplace and encourages others to follow the company's lead and contribute positively to society. Workplace practices that foster an environment that is inclusive can influence attitudes and norms, which can help people understand and accept others more easily. By utilizing Viva Engage, companies can play a vital role in advancing social equality and justice.

Adapting to a Global Workforce: Today, companies must work with employees from different cultures and countries. With Viva Engage, they can bridge the gap by providing a platform that enables organizations to cater to the varying communication styles of their employees. This can include offering content in different languages and accommodating varying time zones. Viva Engage has been designed to cater to the needs of workers in different locations. It ensures that everyone can participate fully.

Driving Business Success: Viva Engage can help businesses succeed by cultivating a productive and innovative workforce that results in improved employee engagement, superior collaboration, and reduced turnover. Viva Engage's inclusive practices can also help boost an organization's competitive edge and improve its organizational performance. While making a positive contribution to society and its employees, businesses can realize their objectives.

Inclusivity is a crucial component of Viva Engage, as it can help foster a productive and supportive work setting. Viva Engage can help companies by promoting an inclusive culture, driving innovation, ensuring equity, and raising employee engagement. The Viva Engage platform facilitates communication, promotes leadership effectiveness, and accommodates diverse perspectives. In addition, it enhances employer branding, tracks inclusivity efforts, and provides constant learning opportunities.

In the Viva Engage community, the company creates a favorable impact and adapts to accommodate the needs of global workers. Viva Engage's ability to foster an inclusive culture and contribute to a more just and equitable society is evidenced by its numerous positive impacts on business success. By prioritizing inclusivity in its communication tools, companies can effectively attract and retain the best talent, innovate, and achieve their strategic goals. Companies can utilize Viva Engage to establish a workplace wherein workers feel respected and appreciated.

Leverage Viva Engage's Built-In Accessibility Features to Improve User Experience

Viva Engage's built-in accessibility tools can help enhance the experience of employees with disabilities. These tools can help ensure that the company's engagement and communication platform is inclusive, giving everyone equal opportunities to utilize it. Here are several ways to utilize these built-in accessibility features effectively:

- **Screen Reader Compatibility**: For those who are visually impaired, Viva Engage offers support for screen readers, which convert text into Braille or speech.

These individuals can then interact with the platform
and navigate. For users who rely on screen readers, Viva
Engage must ensure that all of its content is compatible
with the device. This includes all the documents,
images, and text that are featured on the platform. In
addition, the company should regularly test the system
to ensure that its features are working properly.

- **Keyboard Navigation**: Most people with disabilities,
  including those who have mobility impairments,
  depend on keyboard navigation to navigate Viva
  Engage. Its fully featured design makes use of these
  shortcuts. In addition, educate users about the different
  keyboard shortcuts and teach them how to use them
  efficiently. Make sure that interactive elements, such as
  links and buttons, are also accessible using keyboard
  navigation.

- **Alternative Text for Images**: When reading images,
  screen readers can benefit from the use of alternative
  text, which provides a description of the image.
  This feature is important for those who are visually
  impaired. Employees should be encouraged to include
  descriptive alt text in all images that are submitted
  to Viva Engage. This will ensure that those who are
  visually impaired can get the same information.

- **Captioning and Transcription for Videos**: Providing
  transcripts and captions for videos ensures that hard-
  of-hearing individuals and deaf users can easily access
  the information. Actions include uploading captions
  to Viva Engage and using transcription services to offer
  text versions of audio files. You should also encourage
  the use of live captions during events and meetings.

- **High Contrast Mode:** A high contrast mode can help
  improve readability for those who suffer from visual
  impairments. It increases the contrast between the text
  and the background colors. To ensure that users have
  the proper access to high contrast mode, they should
  be informed about how to enable it in Viva Engage.
  They should also be provided with guidance on how to
  adjust it in their browsers and operating systems.

- **Customizable Text Size:** Enable users to change the
  size of text to help individuals with visual impairments
  easily read content. Make sure that the Viva Engage
  app is responsive and has a smooth and user-friendly
  design. Also, inform users about how to change the size
  of text.

- **Accessible Document Formats:** All documents that
  are shared through Viva Engage should be formatted
  in a way that is accessible. This includes the use of lists,
  headings, and alt text. To make sure that all documents
  are accessible, employees should be trained on how
  to create accessible documents. They should also
  use tools that can help them identify issues with the
  content.

- **Simplified Language and Clear Layouts:** Clear layouts
  and simple language make it easier for people with
  cognitive impairments to understand and use the
  content. In all communications, make sure that the
  language is simple and clear. Organize documents
  logically and avoid using unnecessary jargon.

- **Regular Accessibility Audits**: Viva Engage should conduct regular audits to identify and resolve any accessibility issues. To ensure that Viva Engage complies with accessibility standards, regular audits should be carried out. The company should utilize automated tools and conduct manual tests to evaluate its platform and address any issues immediately.

- **Inclusive Design Practices**: By integrating practices that are inclusive into its development, Viva Engage can continue to improve its accessibility. Through the use of feedback from different groups, the company can identify areas of its platform where it can make improvements.

- **Training and Awareness Programs**: Raising awareness about Viva Engage's accessibility can help all employees become knowledgeable about its importance and how to take advantage of its features. To do this, the company should provide regular training sessions, launch awareness campaigns, and offer support and resources.

- **Accessible Content Guidelines**: The creation of accessible content should be carried out in a manner that ensures consistency across all Viva Engage communications. This can be achieved by establishing guidelines that cover the use of plain language, alt text, and captions. They should also be integrated into workflows to encourage adherence.

143

- **Feedback Mechanisms**: Feedback mechanisms can
  be created to allow users to share their concerns about
  Viva Engage's accessibility. They should also be made
  easier to use. The company should actively encourage
  suggestions and feedback and promptly address
  any issues.

The built-in accessibility tools of Viva Engage play a vital role in making the company's user experience more inclusive. Implementing these features can help ensure that everyone, regardless of their capabilities, can participate in the workplace seamlessly. This approach not only enhances the experience but also promotes respect and inclusivity, fostering a culture of innovation and productivity. Organizations can establish a supportive atmosphere by constantly working toward accessibility.

Viva Engage Compliance to Regulatory Requirements

To comply with various regulations, such as the General Data Protection Regulation (GDPR), the Health Insurance Portability and Accountability Act (HIPAA), and the Service Organization Control 2 (SOC 2), platforms like Viva Engage must ensure that they are following proper procedures. This platform helps organizations foster communication and handle sensitive data. This ensures that the platform is following proper procedures and that the users are protected from legal repercussions. To learn more about how Viva Engage complies with these regulations, please refer to the following detailed overview.

General Data Protection Regulation (GDP)

The General Data Protection Regulation (GDPR) is a European Union law that governs how personal information is collected, stored, and processed. Through its various measures, Viva Engage is able to comply with this regulation as per the official information published on the Microsoft website, which is explained as follows:

- **Data Minimization**: By implementing the principle of minimization of data collection, Viva Engage minimizes the risk of unauthorized access and utilization of the collected information. This ensures that the data is only used for the intended purposes.

- **User Consent**: Viva Engage encourages users to be informed about how their data is being used and stored. This ensures that the company complies with the GDPR. Prior to the processing of their data, users should provide explicit consent.

- **Right to Access and Erasure**: Viva Engage gives users the right to access and remove their personal information. This enables them to do so in a way that's respectful of the GDPR's "right to be forgotten." The platform helps users efficiently accomplish their requests.

- **Data Portability**: The Viva Engage platform also supports data portability, which allows users to reuse and obtain their personal information across various services. This feature is very useful for those who wish to transfer their data without having to go through any additional steps.

- **Data Protection Impact Assessments (DPIAs):** Viva
  Engage also conducts regular data protection impact
  assessments to identify possible risks associated with
  its operations. These evaluations help the company
  align its protection measures with the requirements of
  the GDPR.

- **Encryption and Anonymization**: Viva Engage utilizes
  various methods to protect the privacy of its users'
  data. These include the use of encryption techniques
  when it's in transit and at rest. It also employs
  pseudonymization when needed to safeguard the
  information.

- **Appointment of Data Protection Officer (DPO)**:
  Microsoft, which owns Viva Engage, has appointed
  a Data Protection Officer who is responsible for
  overseeing the company's compliance with the
  GDPR. This individual monitors the activities of the
  company's data processing department and handles
  inquiries related to the use of the platform.

Health Insurance Portability and Accountability Act (HIPAA)

The Health Insurance Portability and Accountability Act of 1996 (HIPAA)
is a federal regulation that governs the protection of health data. Although
Viva Engage isn't designed to provide healthcare-specific features, it
can still be used in settings where sensitive information is involved. This
means that HIPAA compliance is important.

- **Protected Health Information (PHI) Safeguards**:
  Viva Engage's measures to protect PHI include
  regular audits and strict access controls. This
  ensures that sensitive information is protected from
  unauthorized access.

- **Encryption and Secure Communication**: To comply
  with the HIPAA regulations, Viva Engage utilizes robust
  encryption protocols when sending and receiving
  sensitive information. This ensures that the exchange
  of health data is secure and private.

- **Access Controls and Authentication**: The Viva Engage
  platform also has robust access controls . These include
  requiring users to use a multifactor authentication to
  verify their identities. This ensures that sensitive data is
  not accessible to unauthorized individuals.

- **Audit Trails and Monitoring**: The Viva Engage
  platform also has extensive audit trails that track all
  activities related to the exchange of health data. These
  reports are regularly reviewed to identify potential
  security issues and prevent unauthorized access.

- **Training and Awareness Programs**: Microsoft also
  provides its employees with regular training on how to
  comply with the HIPAA regulations. This ensures that
  they are aware of the best practices and regulations.

- **Business Associate Agreements (BAAs)**: Through
  its Business Associate Agreements, Microsoft also
  helps organizations establish and safeguard their
  commitments to ensure that they follow HIPAA
  regulations.

Service Organization Control 2 (SOC 2)

The Service Organization Control 2 (SOC 2) is an auditing framework that ensures that service providers maintain the confidentiality, integrity, and availability of their customers' data. By meeting these standards, Viva Engage has demonstrated its commitment to protecting the privacy and confidentiality of its customers:

- **Security**: To protect its customers' information, Viva Engage utilizes a variety of security measures. These include firewalls and intrusion detection systems. These are regularly updated to prevent unauthorized access.

- **Availability**: The Viva Engage platform is designed to meet the high availability requirements of its users. This ensures that they can access the services they need. It includes various features such as redundant and failover mechanisms.

- **Processing Integrity**: Viva Engage ensures that the processing of its customers' data is carried out in a secure and timely manner. It uses a variety of checks and balances to keep its system from experiencing errors.

- **Confidentiality**: In addition to these, Viva Engage also utilizes various measures to protect the sensitive information that it collects. These include strict data handling procedures and access controls.

- **Privacy**: Viva Engage follows privacy policies that specify how the company collects, uses, and disposes of the information that it collects. These policies are bound by international privacy guidelines and are regularly updated.

Integrated Compliance Strategies

The Viva Engage platform features a variety of compliance strategies that help protect the privacy and data of users. These include the following:

- **Regular Audits and Assessments**: The Viva Engage platform undergoes regular external and internal audits to ensure that it is following the latest regulations such as HIPAA, SOC 2, and GDPR. These audits identify areas for improvement and ensure that the platform is in compliance.

- **Incident Response and Management**: In addition to regular internal audits, the Viva Engage platform also has an incident response plan that is designed to address security and data breaches. This plan includes various steps that can be taken to prevent and minimize the impact of these incidents.

- **User Education and Awareness**: Microsoft also conducts awareness programs to educate its users about various regulations and data protection practices. These programs are designed to help keep them informed about their roles in maintaining the platform's compliance.

- **Data Protection by Design and Default**: When it comes to protecting the privacy and security of its users, the Viva Engage platform uses design principles in its development and design processes. This approach ensures that the security and privacy of its users are considered from the beginning.

- **Collaboration with Regulatory Bodies:** Through its
  collaboration with regulatory bodies, Microsoft updates
  its Viva Engage platform on the latest regulations and
  best practices. This helps ensure that it is following the
  latest legislation.

The conclusion is that the Viva Engage platform follows the latest
regulations set by HIPAA, GDPR, and SOC 2. These regulations help
ensure that the company is following proper procedures and protecting
the privacy and data of its users. By implementing effective measures,
the platform is able to create a secure environment for its users. The
company's continuous efforts to ensure that its platform is following the
latest regulations help it maintain a culture of compliance and security,
which can benefit its users and other stakeholders.

Security Features and Controls in Viva Engage: Data Encryption, Access Controls, and Identity Management

The Microsoft Viva Engage platform is designed to help organizations
create and manage effective collaboration and engagement. It offers a
variety of security controls and features to protect sensitive data. This
overview looks into the security aspects of this platform, focusing on
identity management, data encryption, and access controls.

- **Data Encryption:** When it comes to protecting
  sensitive data, it is important that the information is
  protected from unauthorized access. With the help of
  encryption, the Viva Engage platform can ensure that
  the data is kept secure both at rest and during transit.

- **Encryption at Rest**: The Viva Engage platform
  uses the Advanced Encryption Standard (AES) 256
  encryption standard to protect its servers' data. This
  ensures that the information remains secure even if an
  unauthorized user tries to access it. Key management is
  handled through a secure system. Microsoft uses strict
  access controls and regular key rotation to protect the
  keys against unauthorized access.

- **Encryption in Transit**: The data sent and received by
  the Viva Engage platform through devices is encrypted
  using the Transport Layer Security protocol, which
  prevents unauthorized access and eavesdropping. All
  the APIs used by the Viva Engage platform are secured
  by using the Transport Layer Security (TLS) protocol.
  This ensures that the data sent and received between
  various applications and services is protected.

- **Access Controls**: One of the most critical factors
  that organizations should consider when it comes to
  protecting their data is the availability of limited access
  controls. With the ability to manage user permissions,
  the Viva Engage app can help them create and manage
  their own policies.

- **Role-Based Access Control (RBAC)**: The ability to
  assign user permissions based on their roles is known
  as RBAC. This feature helps prevent unauthorized
  access by restricting the access that users have to the
  specific data and features that they need. The Viva
  Engage app has predefined roles for various groups,
  such as the Moderator, Member, and Admin. These

roles have specific permissions that are designed to
accommodate varying responsibilities and access
levels. Viva Engage's custom role feature allows
administrators to create their own unique roles to meet
specific organizational requirements.

- **Conditional Access Policies**: One of the most effective
  ways to protect the data that the Viva Engage app
  collects is through multifactor authentication. This
  feature requires users to use various methods to verify
  their identity. This type of security measure helps
  prevent unauthorized access. The ability to restrict
  access to Viva Engage can be based on the device
  compliance policies of the company. This feature
  helps prevent unauthorized access and minimize
  the risk of data breaches caused by compromised
  devices. Another type of security measure that can
  be used to enhance the security of the Viva Engage
  app is location-based access. This feature allows
  organizations to restrict the access to the platform from
  certain locations.

- **Data Loss Prevention (DLP)**: In addition, the DLP
  policies of Viva Engage can be used to scan the
  content of the company's app for sensitive data, such
  as personal information and credit card numbers.
  Whenever sensitive data is detected, protective
  measures are implemented. The automated actions of
  the DLP can block, encrypt, and notify users whenever
  sensitive information is found, thereby preventing
  intentional or accidental leaks.

- **Identity Management**: An effective identity
  management solution helps ensure that the identities
  of users are secure. Viva Engage works seamlessly
  with Microsoft Azure AD, which provides additional
  features.

- **Integration with Azure Active Directory (AAD)**: One
  of the most important features of Viva Engage is its
  integration with AAD, which allows users to access the
  platform using their existing credentials. This feature
  eliminates the need for them to create a new password
  and improves the login process. AAD simplifies the
  process of creating and managing user accounts.
  It ensures that inactive accounts are disabled or
  managed properly, which can minimize the likelihood
  of unauthorized access. AAD also supports group
  management, which enables administrators to create
  and control groups of users. This feature helps simplify
  the allocation of permissions and establishes consistent
  access restrictions across the organization.

- **Identity Protection**: AAD uses machine learning to
  analyze and respond to sign-in activities, and it can then
  apply conditional access policies according to the level
  of risk involved. This method provides a more adaptive
  security approach. An identity governance feature can
  be used to ensure that the access of users is regularly
  checked and verified. This can help prevent unauthorized
  access and maintain the appropriate permissions.
  Privileged identity management, or PIM, is a type of
  security that monitors and secures access to critical
  assets. It allows just-in-time access to privileged roles,
  and it requires prior approval for sensitive activities.

153

- **Compliance and Auditing**: Viva Engage maintains
  audit logs that detail every activity of its users. These
  logs can be used to provide forensic and compliance
  investigators with insight into who has access to the
  information. Viva Engage has been certified to comply
  with various regulations, such as the Health Insurance
  Portability and Accountability Act of 1996 (HIPAA),
  the General Data Protection Regulation (GDPR), and
  ISO 27001. These certifications help ensure that the
  platform follows strict privacy and security guidelines.

- **Secure Collaboration**: Protected channels are
  included with Viva Engage to ensure secure
  communication. These channels are only accessible
  to authorized users. The information barrier feature
  blocks certain users from communicating with others.
  This function can help prevent conflicts of interest and
  comply with regulations. External users can securely
  work together using the platform's guest access feature.
  Accounts for guests are protected by the same security
  measures as those for internal users.

The Microsoft Viva Engage platform has numerous security features
that help protect sensitive data and ensure secure collaboration and
communication. These include granular access controls, encryption, and
identity management. These capabilities can help organizations enhance
worker engagement and keep their environment compliant.

Future of Viva Engage Platform

As the evolution of the digital workplace continues, Microsoft's Viva
Engage platform is set to undergo significant changes. It is designed to help
organizations improve their culture and enhance employee engagement.

In this section, we will discuss my personal experience with Yammer and now Viva Engage and how it will affect the modern workplace.

Strategic Direction: In the future, Viva Engage will likely have more advanced capabilities that will allow it to customize its interactions and content based on the users' past and current activities. This approach will make the platform more engaging and relevant. In addition, the platform will also be able to introduce more interactive features, such as live polls and live Q&A sessions. These will allow employees to participate in more meaningful conversations. Further, Viva Engage will be able to integrate even more third-party applications and Microsoft products, which will make it easier for employees to access various resources and tools. Through the enhanced APIs, companies can extend and customize the Viva Engage platform to meet their specific needs. This will allow them to integrate custom solutions and workflows.

Through the enhanced APIs, companies can extend and customize the Viva Engage platform to meet their specific needs. This will allow them to integrate custom solutions and workflows.

In the future, Viva Engage will undergo a radical transformation, becoming progressively more focused on advanced analytics, which will offer companies unparalleled insight into their employee sentiment, health, and overall corporate culture. Viva Engage will focus on delivering actionable insights, which can help HR professionals and managers make informed decisions regarding the improvement of their employees' productivity and experience.

Technological Advancements: Artificial intelligence (AI) is expected to play a vital role in the future, as it will be able to predict a user's needs and provide recommendations that will help them find the most relevant content. New capabilities for natural language processing (NLP) will allow communication tools to become more intuitive and natural. Virtual assistants and chatbots will also become more advanced, allowing users to access information quickly and navigate the platform.

In the future, the integration of augmented and virtual reality will allow employees to interact with the platform in new and engaging ways. For instance, virtual training sessions and meetings can be conducted in a completely immersive manner. The use of these technologies will allow remote workers to collaborate and engage in new and innovative ways, making it easier for them to carry out their work.

In the future, adopting a Zero Trust architecture will allow organizations to thoroughly vet every access request, regardless of its originating point. This approach will help protect sensitive data and enhance security. Continuous updates to the privacy features of the platform will help ensure that it complies with the latest regulations such as the Health Insurance Portability and Accountability Act of 1996 (HIPAA) and the General Data Protection Regulation (GDPR).

Broader Implications for the Modern Workplace: The flexibility of the Viva Engage platform will allow organizations to create and manage hybrid work environments that are ideal for both remote and on-site workers. The digital well-being features of the Viva Engage platform will help employees improve their personal well-being and manage their work life more effectively.

Viva Engage will also help organizations establish strong communities by connecting workers across various departments and regions. This approach will foster a sense of inclusivity and belonging, which is important for maintaining a positive culture. The Viva Engage platform will focus on enhancing tools that enable feedback and recognition, fostering a culture of continuous improvement and appreciation.

Viva Engage will integrate with various learning platforms, including those used for professional development and continuous learning, to help promote professional growth and improve the skills of employees. Viva Engage will help individuals develop their careers by connecting them with mentors and allowing them to see potential job paths within the firm.

Future Features and Enhancements: In the future, the ability to work on projects and documents in real time will be an integral part of the Viva Engage platform. This will allow users to improve their productivity and collaborate more effectively. Furthermore, in the future, the Viva Engage platform should be able to work seamlessly across different operating systems and devices. Doing so will help maintain flexibility and accessibility.

We will also see a centralized knowledge hub that will be able to help employees easily access and share information, which will foster a culture of continuous learning and knowledge sharing. Finally, Viva Engage will be able to provide users with an enhanced search experience, powered by artificial intelligence. This will allow them to find the information they require, even in complex datasets.

Viva Engage's continuous improvements will be able to make its platform easier to use, lowering the learning curve and increasing the adoption rate. As the number of people using mobile devices continues to rise, it is important that the Viva Engage platform is optimized for them. This will allow it to provide a better user experience on tablets and smartphones.

Challenges and Considerations

Due to the evolution of cyber threats, it is important that organizations continuously invest in their cybersecurity efforts to protect their sensitive data. In order to comply with varying regulations, organizations must constantly adapt to the changes.

Change management is also important in order to encourage user engagement and adoption. It can be done through the development of various strategies such as training and support. One of the most important factors that an organization must consider when it comes to implementing the Viva Engage platform is the measurement of its impact on employee productivity and engagement.

When it comes to introducing new features, it's important to strike a balance between innovation and usability so that the Viva Engage platform remains simple and accessible to everyone. One of the most crucial factors an organization must consider is the inclusion of user feedback. Regularly soliciting their suggestions will ensure that the Viva Engage platform continues to evolve in line with the needs of its users.

Viva Engage's future is bright as it continues to adapt to the workplace's evolving needs. By integrating cutting-edge technologies like virtual reality, augmented reality, and security protocols, it can become a vital part of any organization's communication strategy. Its commitment to providing a secure and easy-to-use platform, as well as its emphasis on employee productivity and privacy, will ensure its continued existence.

As organizations look to adopt hybrid work methods and prioritize the well-being of their employees, Viva Engage will play a vital role in helping them foster a productive and connected workforce. By constantly adapting to the changes brought about by the new landscape, Viva Engage will be able to help organizations create an improved culture that encourages growth and development.

Viva Engage will continue to develop through its continuous focus on improving its user experience and delivering on its promise of creating an engaging and connected workplace. This will help boost employee satisfaction and business success.

With this, we have come to the conclusion of this last chapter where we have seen the importance of accessibility and inclusivity in digital platforms like Viva Engage and its impact on diverse user groups; highlighted built-in accessibility features within Viva Engage and how they can be leveraged to improve user experience for all; discussed various compliance regulations and standards that may apply to organizations using Viva Engage, such as GDPR, HIPAA, and S OC 2; and explored the security features and controls available within Viva Engage, including data encryption, access controls, and identity management. Also, a personal view and recommendations have been covered on the future of the Viva Engage platform.

Hope you had a great experience reading this book, and closing with an expectation that it will benefit you in the Viva Engage implementation in your organization. Please send any feedback to `charles.waghmare@gmail.com`.

Index

© The Editor(s) (if applicable) and The Author(s),
under exclusive license to APress Media, LLC, part of Springer Nature 2024
C. Waghmare, *Engage, Excel, and Elevate with Microsoft Viva Engage*, Apress Pocket Guides,
https://doi.org/10.1007/979-8-8688-0766-4

W, X, Y, Z